Idioms
and Other English Expressions

Developed by
Timothy Rasinski

It's raining cats and dogs!

Author

Kathleen Knoblock

SHELL EDUCATION

Editor
Lisa Greathouse

Creative Director
Lee Aucoin

Assistant Editor
Leslie Huber, M.A.

Cover Design
Lee Aucoin

Editorial Director
Dona Herweck Rice

Illustration Manager/ Designer
Timothy J. Bradley

Editor-in-Chief
Sharon Coan, M.S.Ed.

Interior Layout Design and Print Production
Robin Erickson

Editorial Manager
Gisela Lee, M.A.

Publisher
Corinne Burton, M.A.Ed

Shell Education
5301 Oceanus Drive
Huntington Beach, CA 92649-1030
http://www.shelleducation.com
ISBN 978-1-4258-0158-8
© 2008 Shell Education
Reprinted 2009

Table of Contents

The No Child Left Behind (NCLB) legislation mandates that all states adopt academic standards that identify the skills students will learn in kindergarten through grade 12. While many states had already adopted academic standards prior to NCLB, the legislation set requirements to ensure the standards are detailed and comprehensive.

Standards are designed to focus instruction and guide adoption of curricula. Standards are statements that describe the criteria necessary for students to meet specific academic goals. They define the knowledge, skills, and content students should acquire at each level. Standards are also used to develop standardized tests to evaluate students' academic progress.

In many states today, teachers are required to demonstrate how their lessons meet state standards. State standards are used in the development of Shell Education products; therefore, educators can be assured that they meet the academic requirements of each state.

How to Find Your State Correlations

Shell Education is committed to producing educational materials that are research and standards based. In this effort, all products are correlated to the academic standards of the 50 states, the District of Columbia, and the Department of Defense Dependent Schools. A correlation report customized for your state can be printed directly from the following website: *http://www.shelleducation.com*. If you require assistance in printing correlation reports, please contact Customer Service at 1-877-777-3450.

McREL Compendium

Shell Education uses the Mid-continent Research for Education and Learning (McREL) Compendium to create standards correlations. Each year, McREL analyzes state standards and revises the compendium. By following this procedure, they are able to produce a general compilation of national standards.

All of the following McREL standards apply to each lesson in this book.

McREL Standard, Level, and Benchmark	Standard
Reading 5.I.1	The student uses mental images based on pictures and print to aid in comprehension of text.
Reading 5.I.6	The student understands level-appropriate sight words and reading vocabulary.
Reading 5.I.8	The student reads aloud familiar stories, poems, and passages with fluency and expression (e.g., rhythm, flow, meter, tempo, pitch, tone, intonation).
Reading 5.II.1	The student previews text (e.g., skims material; uses pictures, textual clues, and text format).
Reading 5.II.3	The student makes, confirms, and revises simple predictions about what will be found in a text (e.g., uses prior knowledge and ideas presented in text, illustrations, titles, topic sentences, key words, and foreshadowing clues).
Reading 5.II.6	The student uses word reference materials to determine the meaning, pronunciation, and derivations of unknown words.
Reading 6.II.7	The student understands the ways in which language is used in literary texts (e.g., personification, alliteration, onomatopoeia, simile, metaphor, imagery, hyperbole, rhythm).
Writing 1.I.2	The student uses strategies to draft and revise written work.
Writing 1.I.8	The student writes for different purposes (e.g., to entertain, inform, learn, communicate ideas).

The National Reading Panel (2000) has identified vocabulary as an essential component of effective literacy instruction. When students don't know the meanings of the words and phrases in the texts they read, they are likely to experience difficulty in sufficiently understanding those very same texts.

Some of the most difficult vocabulary to understand are those words and phrases that don't reflect their literal meanings—idioms. Idioms are words that are essentially metaphorical in nature (Harris & Hodges, 1995; Riccio, 1980). When a person writes "It's raining cats and dogs," he or she does not mean that dogs and cats are literally falling out of the sky, but that it is raining hard. When another writes "Birds of a feather…," he or she is referring most likely to a group of people with common interests or characteristics, and not animals that fly.

Idioms and figurative language are part and parcel of oral and written language. English is rich in idioms (Harris & Hodges, 1995). Petrosky (1980) estimates that adults may use over a half million figures of speech over the course of a year.

Because English is so filled with idioms, it can be difficult to understand (Blachowicz & Fisher, 2002) and translate into another language (Harris & Hodges, 1995). All of us at one time or another have come across a figure of speech that we don't quite understand because we have not been previously exposed to it and were not told the meaning of the phrase or given sufficient clues to make sense of it. Children, by their very nature of having limited life experiences, are more likely to encounter figurative language that they do not understand. This is especially true of English language learners who have had even less exposure to experiences involving the English language.

The use of idioms and other forms of figurative language in writing is a characteristic of high-quality literature (Blachowicz & Fisher, 2002). Authors include idioms in their writing to clarify their message and make their message more interesting for readers. "Figurative language uses comparisons, contrasts, and unusual juxtapositions of words to draw our attention to aspect of the world we live in" (Blachowicz & Fisher, 2002, p. 79). However, if a reader is unfamiliar with the idioms in the text, he or she is likely to have a poor or limited understanding of the text.

Thus, the study of idioms is certainly worthwhile, as great awareness and understanding of idiomatic language can enhance students' understanding of the texts they are asked to read. Yet, most core reading programs do not provide sufficient instructional coverage on idioms and other forms of figurative language. Thus, *Idioms and Other English Expressions* has been developed as a means to provide specific and engaging instruction on idiomatic language for students. As students become more acquainted with idioms, reading comprehension will improve.

The major intent of this program, then, is to improve students' reading comprehension and overall reading achievement. However, as noted above, high-quality writing is marked by the use of idioms and other forms of figurative language. Thus, students' writing is a second beneficiary of the use of this instructional program. As students' knowledge and use of idiomatic language improve, the quality of their writing will likely show measurable gains as well.

Idioms and Other English Expressions was designed to make word study fun for students. So, when it comes to teaching vocabulary, don't sit on the fence, don't have cold feet, and don't try to pull any strings. Let me do the honors and make heads and tails out of teaching idiomatic vocabulary for your students. Before you know it, you'll be standing on your own two feet, teaching idioms will be as comfortable as an old shoe, and your students will be head over heels in love with idioms for reading and writing.

Best wishes,

Timothy Rasinski

References and Resources

Blachowicz, C., and P. Fisher. 2002. *Teaching vocabulary in all classrooms.* 2nd ed. Columbus: Merrill/Prentice-Hall.

Fry, E. 2002. *The vocabulary teacher's book of lists.* San Francisco: Jossey-Bass.

Fry, E., and J. Kress. 2006. *The reading teacher's book of lists.* San Francisco: Jossey-Bass.

Harris, T. L., and R. E. Hodges, eds. 1995. *The literacy dictionary: The vocabulary of reading and writing.* Newark, DE: International Reading Association.

Johnson, D. D. 2001. *Vocabulary in the elementary and middle school.* Boston: Allyn & Bacon.

National Reading Panel. 2000. *The report of the National Reading Panel.* Washington, DC: U.S. Department of Education.

Newton, E., N. Padak, and T. Rasinski. 2007. *Evidence-based instruction in reading: A professional development guide to vocabulary (Evidence-Based Instruction in Reading).* Boston: Allyn & Bacon.

Petrosky, A. R. 1980. *The inferences we make: Children and literature. Language Arts* 57: 149–156.

Riccio, O. M. 1980. *The intimate art of writing poetry.* Englewood Cliffs, NJ: Prentice-Hall.

Idioms and other expressions are tricky to understand for native English speakers. They can be especially challenging for students who are English language learners. Here are a few ideas you can use with any students who would benefit from scaffolding activities to help them comprehend nonliteral expressions.

Make Connections With Oral Language Experience

Offer students several situations that they would likely have experienced universally. Use a few from the list below and add your own. Present a situation and complete it yourself as a model. Example: Once I ate too much at dinner and I felt like (*a stuffed pig, I'd eaten an elephant, a giant meatball*). Then, ask a number of students to think of another way to complete the situation. Encourage students to be expressive. Accept all answers. If needed, you can prompt them by asking such questions as, "In this situation, would you feel more like a stuffed pig or as skinny as a rail?" If you like, record some of the students' responses on the board or on chart paper. At the end of the activity, ask students to identify and read the response they gave.

1. I remember a time that I was as scared as…
2. Having a friend is like…
3. One time I was as sick as…
4. I remember a time that I was as mad as…

5. Once I tried a food that was more disgusting than…
6. A flower is as beautiful as…
7. I got so wet in the rain that I looked like…
8. One time I laughed so hard that…

Make a Literal vs. Figurative Mini-Book of Idioms and Other Expressions

Have students use several sheets of drawing or story paper to make a blank booklet. Instruct them to create a title page for the cover. Then, on each two-page spread, have students illustrate pictures of the literal and figurative meanings of an idiom or other expression. Ask them to label their literal interpretation "What It Says" and their figurative interpretation "What It Means." At the bottom, have them write the expression and what it really means. You may want to model this for students using an example such as the one shown in the illustration.

What It Says	What It Means
Hold your horses!	Slow down. Wait.

Expressing Feelings with Idioms

To familiarize students with how idioms can express feelings, play a game of "How Would *You* Feel?" Choose an idiom from the list on pages 14–17 (for example, *seeing red*). Give students a brief scenario using the idiom. (Jena saw her sister at school wearing Jena's favorite sweater. When she realized that her sister had taken it from her room, she began seeing red.) Ask students how they would feel and to identify the feeling being expressed, such as *mad, sad, happy*, or *scared*. Then ask students what phrase expresses that feeling. Repeat the phrase and the feeling. (Yes, Jena was mad. She was seeing red.)

Name _____ Date _____

I Spy Idioms and Other Expressions

I have been on the lookout for idioms and other expressions. Below are ones I saw or heard.

Expression: _____

What It Means: _____

Where I Saw or Heard It: _____

Expression: _____

What It Means: _____

Where I Saw or Heard It: _____

Expression: _____

What It Means: _____

Where I Saw or Heard It: _____

Expression: _____

What It Means: _____

Where I Saw or Heard It: _____

Expression: _____

What It Means: _____

Where I Saw or Heard It: _____

Where Did That Saying Come From?

Possible Origins of Idioms and Other Expressions

Have you ever heard an expression and wondered where it might have come from or how it got started? Here are some common expressions and their possible origins, or beginnings.

1. *I went to the store to buy a toy I saw advertised on sale, but they had no more left. The manager gave me a* **rain check**.

The term *rain check* comes from the game of baseball. In the 1800s, if you had a ticket to a game that wasn't played because of rain, then you got a ticket for another game in the future. This was known as a rain check. Today, a rain check is a piece of paper that says you can get an item that is sold out now some time in the future at the price it was advertised.

2. *Daryl was very sick. The doctor said that he was getting better, but that he was not* **out of the woods** *yet.*

Years ago, people thought of the woods as a dark, scary place where danger lurked. To be out of the woods *meant that you were safe. The saying came to mean free from worry or danger about a scary or dangerous situation.*

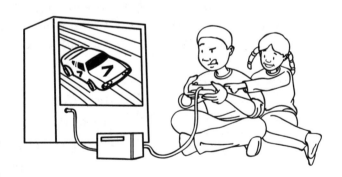

3. *Natalie taught her dad how to play a video game, but it took all afternoon before he* **got a handle on it.**

Imagine trying to lift a big heavy box with no handles. It seems impossible. However, if it has handles, it may still be difficult, but it is much more manageable because you have something to grip. To *get a handle* on something means to take control of or find a way to manage something difficult. This expression is related to *get a grip*.

Where Did That Saying Come From? *(cont.)*

4. Bobby had three pages of math homework. When his mom came to check on him, he hadn't started yet. "**Stop beating around the bush!**" she said.

Have you ever tried to avoid doing something by finding other things to do first? You need to be coaxed to get going on it. The expression *beating around the bush* comes from the 1500s. Hunters would hire people to beat sticks around the bushes to coax the animals out from hiding. Today, this expression means to put off facing something or to come to it in a roundabout way.

5. Colin and Tony had been best friends as long as they could remember. They were the same age, liked the same things, and even dressed alike. Their moms said that they were **like peas in a pod**.

If you looked at green peas, even closely, it would be hard to tell one from another. A pod is the name of the casing around peas. Inside the pod, the peas grow side-by-side in a row and look almost identical in size, shape, and color. The expression *like peas in a pod* means alike in many ways.

6. When my baby cousin thought a bag of dog biscuits were cookies, I couldn't **keep a straight face**.

What happens to your face when you laugh out loud? Your mouth opens wide, your eyes squint, and your face wrinkles up. It certainly doesn't keep straight! The expression keep a straight face means don't laugh.

7. I like going to my Aunt Caroline's house to visit. She has a garden full of flowers and vegetables. When I grow up I'd like to have a garden and **a green thumb** like Aunt Caroline.

People who garden use their hands to handle plants. The parts of plants that are green contain a chemical called chlorophyll. When someone handles the leaves and stems of plants, some of the green color can rub off onto their hands. Someone who has *a green thumb* then is considered to be good at growing plants.

My Top Five Favorite Expressions

Name _____ **Date** _____

What idioms or other expressions really *tickle you pink*? In other words, what are your favorites?
Think about expressions you have heard, read, or learned. Choose and write five that you
especially like. Then, in the stars, rank them with the numbers 1–5 in order from least to most
favorite. Finally, put a ✓ in each box when you hear, say, read, or use it in writing.

Idiom or Expression

#

☐ I heard it. ☐ I said it. ☐ I read it. ☐ I wrote it.

#

☐ I heard it. ☐ I said it. ☐ I read it. ☐ I wrote it.

#

☐ I heard it. ☐ I said it. ☐ I read it. ☐ I wrote it.

#

☐ I heard it. ☐ I said it. ☐ I read it. ☐ I wrote it.

#

☐ I heard it. ☐ I said it. ☐ I read it. ☐ I wrote it.

A Little Thesaurus of Idioms

What is the difference between reading something boring and something interesting? In many cases, it is the words that the writer chooses to describe something or tell the story. Writers sometimes use a special book to help them pick just the right words for what they want to say. This book is called a *thesaurus*. A thesaurus lists words related to one another in meaning. For example, under the word *fast*, you might find *quick, speedy,* and *swift*. These words are fine, but you could also describe *fast* with an idiom, such as *in a flash, as quick as a wink,* or *in a jiffy*. Below are some words you probably use often in your speaking and writing. Next to each one are some idioms you could choose to use instead to make your sentences more interesting.

Ho-Hum Word	Idioms You Might Use Instead	
happy	walking on air in good spirits flying high	on cloud nine on top of the world as happy as a clam
sad	down in the dumps feeling blue moping around	have the blues brokenhearted in the doldrums
mad	seeing red burned up in a huff	steaming fit to be tied as mad as a hornet
surprised	bowled over caught off guard hit me like a ton of bricks	taken aback stunned

In Other Words

Name _____ **Date** _____

Do you often read or use the words *happy*, *sad*, *mad*, or *surprised*? These words describe feelings, but are not very interesting. You have learned that idioms and other expressions can be used to describe things in a more interesting way. Read each description below. Focus on the ho-hum word in bold. Then, look at the underlined sentence. Use your idiom thesaurus on page 12 or your own ideas to revise, or put it in other words. Write your new sentence on the lines.

1. It was early morning. Mr. Smith arrived a little late to open his store. When he put his key in to unlock the door, it broke in the lock. Mr. Smith could not open the store on time. <u>He was **mad**.</u> Now he would have to call a locksmith and wait for him to come.

   _____

   _____

2. Jennifer sat in the dentist's chair. Dr. Chu had taken X-rays of her teeth. She was worried that she might have a cavity and that she would need to get a filling. Dr. Chu looked carefully at the X-rays and said, "Hmmm." Then he told Jennifer that she had been doing a good job taking care of her teeth. She had no cavities. <u>Jennifer was **happy**.</u>

   _____

   _____

3. Mrs. Jackson came into Bobby's room. She said that she had some news. Someone at work had given her tickets to the hockey playoffs. Bobby never expected to be able to see a hockey game live. <u>Bobby was **surprised**</u>.

   _____

   _____

4. Andrea and her father got a box and put an old towel in it. They carefully picked up the bird that had fallen from its nest and put it in the box. Dad went back to get a ladder. They were going to try to put it back in the nest. But, when Dad got back, it was too late. The baby bird didn't make it. <u>Andrea was **sad**</u>.

   _____

   _____

Idioms and Other Expressions:
A Reference List for Readers and Writers

Idioms Using Colors

once in a blue moon	feeling blue/got the blues	gray area
out of the blue	has a green thumb	tickled pink
caught red-handed	silver lining	golden days
red-faced	green with envy	in the black
red-carpet treatment	in the pink	seeing red
yellow/yellow-bellied	green-eyed monster	red-letter day

Animal Idioms

let the cat out of the bag	bright-eyed and bushy-tailed	fish for a compliment
monkey business	go to the dogs	in the doghouse
a whale of a time	bug off	open a can of worms
clam up	as the crow flies	hold your horses
hear a peep	butterflies in one's stomach	high on the hog
bird's eye view	chicken feed	
raining cats and dogs	snake in the grass	

Idioms About Food

piece of cake	takes the cake	take it with a grain of salt
food for thought	just desserts	out to lunch
couch potato	doesn't grow on trees	butter someone up
get chewed out	hot potato	walking on eggshells
eat one's words	proof is in the pudding	in a nutshell
apple of my eye	going bananas	bite off more than one can chew
sweet tooth	bowl of cherries	feel one's oats

Idioms and Other Expressions:
A Reference List for Readers and Writers *(cont.)*

Eye, Ear, and Nose Idioms

eagle-eyed	fall upon deaf ears	follow your nose
nose around	pull the wool over one's eyes	in one ear and out the other
keep one's eyes peeled	didn't bat an eyelash	put one's nose to the grindstone
plain as the nose on one's face	take the red-eye	right under one's nose
lend an ear	eyes in the back of one's head	keep one's nose clean
see eye to eye	more than meets the eye	keep one's nose out

Action Idioms

blow the whistle	saw logs	get to the bottom of it
chill out	get off the hook	beat around the bush
throw in the towel	bury the hatchet	carry the ball
rock the boat	pull oneself together	bite one's tongue
catch you later	draw the line	burn one's bridges
kick the bucket	come out of one's shell	put a cork in it
hold your horses	hit the nail on the head	

Idioms to Get and Keep

get a kick out of it	get one's feet wet	get the show on the road
keep the ball rolling	keep a stiff upper lip	keep it under wraps
keep a lid on it	get over it	get it off one's chest
get under one's skin	get the green light	keep one's cool
keep a straight face	keep it to oneself	keep one's fingers crossed
keep on one's toes	get cold feet	
get the runaround	get you down	

Idioms and Other Expressions: A Reference List for Readers and Writers *(cont.)*

Idioms That Put or Pull

pull a stunt	put one's foot in one's mouth	put one's money where one's mouth is
put one's best foot forward	put someone down	pull a fast one
pull one in	put in a good word	pull the plug
put one's eggs in one basket	put the horse before the cart	pull rank
pull one's leg	pull the rug out from under	put one's finger on it
put it/one to the test	pull some strings	pull it off
put one's foot down	pull up stakes	

Expressions That Are Similes

like two peas in a pod	as quiet as a mouse	as sweet as honey
like pulling teeth	as cold as ice	sings like a bird
as different as night and day	as soft as silk	as hungry as a bear
eats like a horse/pig	like a bump on a log	like music to one's ears
like a fish out of water	like water off a duck's back	as green as grass
as easy as pie	as stiff as a board	fit like a glove
fight like cats and dogs	feel like two cents	

Expressions That Are Metaphors

hit the sack	bag of tricks	in the same boat
stopped cold	a tongue-lashing	hard to swallow
lips are sealed	buttoned his lip	spill the beans
the crack of dawn	in the dark	tower of strength
teacher's pet	back out	two-faced
bottled up	catch off guard	
simmer down	hands are tied	

Idioms and Other Expressions: A Reference List for Readers and Writers *(cont.)*

Expressions That Exaggerate (Hyperbole)

crying one's eyes out

in a split second

up to one's neck

made one's head spin

bursting at the seams

out of this world

a dime a dozen

go through the roof

bored stiff

worth its weight in gold

die of boredom

all thumbs

run/running ragged

all ears

in no time

every trick in the book

die laughing

taking one's head off

back-breaking work

Just Common Sayings (Proverbs)

Two heads are better than one.

Out of sight, out of mind.

Actions speak louder than words.

Look before you leap.

Put your best foot forward.

Don't cry over spilled milk.

Don't put the cart before the horse.

Don't count your chickens before they hatch.

The early bird catches the worm.

Time flies when you are having fun.

Cat got your tongue?

Finders keepers, losers weepers.

A stitch in time saves nine.

Better late than never.

Don't judge a book by its cover.

Caught between a rock and a hard place.

Where there's a will there's a way.

Variety is the spice of life.

Idioms Using Colors

This unit highlights idioms based on colors. Below are two lists of idioms that focus on color words. The first, *Ten to Teach*, presents the 10 expressions introduced and taught in this unit. The second, *More to Mention*, offers additional expressions in this theme that you may want to mention or use to create additional activities.

Ten to Teach

1. once in a blue moon
2. out of the blue
3. caught red-handed
4. red-faced
5. green with envy

6. green-eyed monster
7. tickled pink
8. red-carpet treatment
9. looking/feeling blue
10. silver lining

More to Mention

▶ has a green thumb
▶ red-letter day
▶ in the pink

▶ golden days
▶ seeing red
▶ yellow/yellow-bellied

▶ got the blues
▶ in the black
▶ gray area

Using This Unit

Begin by reading to students the basic *Ten to Teach* idioms. Ask students if they have ever heard or used any of these expressions, and if so, how and where. Next, tell students that you are going to read the expressions again, and this time they are to listen for anything they have in common. Accept all answers, and then point out that all of the expressions use color words. Teach or review the definition of an *idiom*—an expression that means something other than what the words actually say. If you like, read the list a third time and let students speculate on what each idiom might really mean.

On the next page is a story that includes the *Ten to Teach* idioms. Note that the story is not intended to be an example of good writing; it would not be natural to use 10 idioms in such a short piece. The purpose of the story is simply to use all the expressions in context. The story is at approximately a 2.2 reading level. Use this information to read it aloud to students, have them read it, or both. This reproducible page includes the story and questions for students to answer related to the idioms used.

The final five pages of the unit introduce the basic *Ten to Teach* idioms individually, two to a page. These can be reproduced as is, or cut apart into separate cards. Use these after the story to reinforce the meanings of the idioms or to test students' understanding of them. Or, use them before the story as preparation for reading or for scaffolding as needed.

Optional: Use one of the ideas or activities in the introductory section of this book as an extension or follow-up to the unit.

Idioms Using Colors (cont.)

Name _____ Date _____

Below is a story that includes 10 idioms using colors. Can you tell what they mean?

The Green-Eyed Monster

I always bring in the mail for my family. I guess I wish that just **once in a blue moon** there were something for me. Last week, a letter came for my big sister. It looked important. I was carefully looking at her letter to see if I could tell what it was, when she appeared **out of the blue**.

"What are you doing, Billy?" she said. "Reading other people's mail is a crime! I **caught you red-handed!**"

"Uh, I wasn't *reading* it," I answered a bit **red-faced**. I was just *looking* at it."

"Well, I'm waiting to hear if I won the **Red-Letter Day** contest. If I do, then I get to go to the Eight Flags Amusement Park all day for free."

Suddenly, I was **green with envy**. The letter in my hand was from Eight Flags. I handed it to my sister. She tore it open. She won. She actually won. The **green-eyed monster** in me wished she hadn't. While she was **tickled pink**, I felt as if a dark cloud formed over my head.

"Listen," she exclaimed. "I'm really going to get the **red-carpet treatment**. They are going to send a limousine to pick me up. And, look! I get to bring a guest, too!"

"Great," I said, not meaning it at all.

"Oh, stop **looking so blue**, silly. Of course I wouldn't pick anyone but you to bring as my guest."

Suddenly, that dark cloud had a **silver lining**. I was going to Eight Flags, too!

Read or listen to the story again. Then answer these questions about the idioms. To help you find them, the idioms are in **dark print** in the story.

1. What color seems to go with feeling sad? _____

2. Is *once in a blue moon* a short time or a long time? _____

3. If you are *red-faced*, are you embarrassed or shy? _____

4. Would you like to get the *red-carpet treatment*?   Explain why or why not. _____

   _____

5. If something came *out of the blue*, were you expecting it or not? _____

   _____

Idioms Using Colors *(cont.)*

Name _____   Date _____

Idiom ▶ **once in a blue moon**

Meaning ▶ **not very often; hardly ever occurring**

How It Is Used ▶ Keri got a bat and ball for his birthday. His dad has taken him out to practice every weekend for several weeks. Dad pitches the ball over and over, but Keri only hits it **once in a blue moon**.

Which Is Right? ▶ Read the two selections. Choose the one in which **once in a blue moon** is used as an idiom. Circle the number of your choice.

❶ Anne likes to watch the night sky. Sometimes the moon is bright and clear. Sometimes it looks hazy and blue. She imagines seeing faces in the moon. She thought she saw a face *once in a blue moon.*

❷ Although he is very busy with work, Mr. Jefferson tries to make time to be with his children. Only *once in a blue moon* is he unable to spend Saturdays with them.

Idiom ▶ **out of the blue**

Meaning ▶ **not expected; seeming to appear from nowhere**

How It Is Used ▶ Karen and her friend Sherry had a disagreement and weren't speaking to each other. After a week, Karen thought she might have lost her friend forever. Then, **out of the blue**, the phone rang and it was Sherry wanting to make up.

Which Is Right? ▶ Read the two selections. Choose the one in which **out of the blue** is used as an idiom. Circle the number of your choice.

❶ Jared knew he wasn't that good of a speller. He thought he might get a *C* on his report card. Then, *out of the blue*, his teacher pulled him aside. She told him that he was doing *B*-level work.

❷ More than an hour had passed on the boat, but the whale watchers were patient. Finally, someone finally spotted the head of a whale popping *out of the blue* water.

Name _____ Date _____

Idiom ▶ **caught red-handed**

Meaning ▶ **discovered in the act of doing something wrong**

How It Is Used ▶ Denise made two dozen cookies to sell at the school fair. As they were out on the counter cooling, Denise saw her little brother take one. "Ah-ha!" she said. **"I caught you red-handed!"**

Which Is Right? ▶ Read the two selections. Choose the one in which **caught red-handed** is used as an idiom. Circle the number of your choice.

❶ Kenny was letting his 5-year-old brother, Joey, help him repaint his bike red. Joey was supposed to be mixing the paint. When Kenny turned around, he *caught him red-handed*, because Joey was using his hand instead of the mixing stick to stir the paint!

❷ The police arrived at the jewelry store just as the robber was coming out the door. They *caught him red-handed* with a sack full of jewels.

Idiom ▶ **red-faced**

Meaning ▶ **embarrassed**

How It Is Used ▶ Charlene walked into class a little late. Suddenly the whole group began to giggle. Charlene looked down and saw that she was wearing her jacket inside out. "Well, I was in a hurry!" she said, **red-faced**.

Which Is Right? ▶ Read the two selections. Choose the one in which **red-faced** is used as an idiom. Circle the number of your choice.

❶ Miss Jones must have reminded the students to bring their permission slips about 10 times. When she asked for Jeremy's, he said, *red-faced*, "I forgot it."

❷ Jenna was at the county fair with her family. She saw a girl with red flowers painted on her cheeks. Jenna asked the *red-faced* girl where she had her face painted. The girl pointed to a long line of children next to the ferris wheel.

Name _____ Date _____

Idiom ▶ **green with envy**

Meaning ▶ **jealous; feeling envy toward someone's good fortune**

How It Is Used ▶ Jerry liked his old bike. But when his friend got a 10-speed bike for his birthday, Jerry was **green with envy**.

Which Is Right? ▶ Read the two selections. Choose the one in which **green with envy** is used as an idiom. Circle the number of your choice.

❶ Tom and Tim were both up for captain of the team. When Tim was chosen, Tom was *green with envy*.

❷ Caroline and her dad were building a tree house. When it was finished, dad asked what color she would like it to be painted. At the store, Caroline chose the paint called *Green with Envy*.

Idiom ▶ **green-eyed monster**

Meaning ▶ **a strong feeling of jealousy, usually with unkind wishes**

How It Is Used ▶ Diana was shopping with her mom and saw a jacket she wanted, but Mom did not let her get it. The next week at school, Diana saw Trish wearing the jacket. The **green-eyed monster** in Diana made her hope that Trish would lose it somewhere.

Which Is Right? ▶ Read the two selections. Choose the one in which **green-eyed monster** is used as an idiom. Circle the number of your choice.

❶ Jimmy was happy with his old bike until he saw that his friend, Les, got a new one. Suddenly he found himself imagining Les falling off his new bike. He liked Les, but a *green-eyed monster* took over his thoughts for a moment.

❷ Late one night, my little sister crept into my room. When I turned on the light, she said she thought that there was a *green-eyed monster* under her bed.

Name _____ Date _____

Idiom ▶ **tickled pink**

Meaning ▶ **delighted; pleased; happy**

How It Is Used ▶ Teri never expected her poem to win a prize. When her named was called as the winner, she was **tickled pink**.

Which Is Right? ▶ Read the two selections. Choose the one in which **tickled pink** is used as an idiom. Circle the number of your choice.

❶ My little brother is always playing jokes on me. Once I decided to really make him laugh. I wrestled him to the floor and poked him in the ribs until he was *tickled pink*.

❷ We could see that mom had not been having a good day. She was grouchy. We went upstairs and made her a card. When we presented it to her, she was *tickled pink*. The rest of the evening, she wasn't a bit grouchy.

Idiom ▶ **red-carpet treatment**

Meaning ▶ **treated with special importance**

How It Is Used ▶ Miss Jones announced to her class that the mayor was coming to visit their school and talk to some of the students. She reminded the children to be on their best behavior and to give their visitor the **red-carpet treatment**.

Which Is Right? ▶ Read the two selections. Choose the one in which **red-carpet treatment** is used as an idiom. Circle the number of your choice.

❶ Queenie wasn't just any dog. She was a show dog who had won many ribbons. Wherever Queenie went, she was given the *red-carpet treatment*.

❷ After the movie, the theater owner noticed that someone had spilled a soft drink on the rug. It needed to be cleaned and treated with stain remover. He asked one of the workers to give the *red carpet treatment*.

Name _____ Date _____

Idiom ▶ **looking/feeling blue**

Meaning ▶ **looking/feeling sad**

How It Is Used ▶ Barry came into class **looking blue**. When his teacher asked why, he said that his pet hamster escaped and couldn't be found.

Which Is Right? ▶ Read the two selections. Choose the one in which **feeling blue** is used as an idiom. Circle the number of your choice.

❶ Terry studied hard for the test. She was sure she would get almost all 10 questions right. When she saw that she had only gotten five right, Terry went home *feeling blue*.

❷ Gwen and Sara were picking out a new sweater for grandma. Gwen was looking through a stack of red ones. Then she saw Sara at another stack, *feeling blue* ones. "These are really soft," Sara said. "Grandma would prefer one of these, don't you think?"

Idiom ▶ **silver lining**

Meaning ▶ **something good that comes out of something bad**

How It Is Used ▶ Kim had an operation and had to stay in the hospital for two weeks. Although it wasn't fun to be away from home for so long, there was a **silver lining**. While she was there, she made friends with the girl who shared her room.

Which Is Right? ▶ Read the two selections. Choose the one in which **silver lining** is used as an idiom. Circle the number of your choice.

❶ Carl was staring at the full moon. When Dad asked what he saw, Carl said the moon looked like it had a *silver lining*.

❷ Mom was upset when she lost her job. She would have to look for another one and it could take a while. But there was a *silver lining*. While she was working, she never had time to look for a better job. Now she did.

This unit highlights idioms based on animals. Below are two lists of idioms that focus on animals and their characteristics. The first, *Ten to Teach*, presents the 10 expressions introduced and taught in this unit. The second, *More to Mention*, offers additional expressions in this theme that you may want to mention or use to create additional activities.

Ten to Teach

1. **let the cat out of the bag**
2. **clam up**
3. **bright-eyed and bushy-tailed**
4. **bugged/bug off**
5. **butterflies in one's stomach**
6. **snake in the grass**
7. **in the doghouse**
8. **hold your horses**
9. **monkey business**
10. **hear a peep**

More to Mention

- ▶ go to the dogs
- ▶ chicken feed
- ▶ as the crow flies
- ▶ fish for a compliment
- ▶ open a can of worms
- ▶ high on the hog
- ▶ a whale of a time
- ▶ bird's eye view
- ▶ raining cats and dogs

Using This Unit

Begin by reading to students the basic *Ten to Teach* idioms. First, ask students if they have ever heard or used any of these expressions, and if so, how and where. Next, tell the students that you are going to read the expressions again, and this time they are to listen for anything they have in common. Accept all answers, and then point out that all the expressions refer to animals. Teach or review the definition of an *idiom*—an expression that means something other than what the words actually say. If you like, read the list a third time and let students speculate on what each idiom might really mean.

On the next page is a story that includes the *Ten to Teach* idioms. Note that the story is not intended to be an example of good writing; it would not be natural to use 10 idioms in such a short piece. The purpose of the story is simply to use all the expressions in context. The story is at approximately a 1.5 reading level. Use this information to read it aloud to students, have them read it, or both. This reproducible page includes the story and questions for students to answer related to the idioms used.

The final five pages of the unit introduce the basic *Ten to Teach* idioms individually, two to a page. These can be reproduced as is, or cut apart into separate cards. Use these after the story to reinforce the meanings of the idioms or to test students' understanding of them. Or, use them before the story as preparation for reading or for scaffolding as needed.

Optional: Use one of the ideas or activities in the introductory section of this book as an extension or follow-up to the unit.

Animal Idioms (cont.)

Name _____   Date _____

Below is a story that includes 10 animal idioms. Can you tell what they mean?

Yippee!

I've wanted to have a sleepover since just about forever. Finally, just before my seventh birthday, my sister **let the cat out of the bag**. My parents were going to let me have a sleepover for my birthday. My sister told me to **clam up** about it, but I went right to my mom, all **bright-eyed and bushy-tailed**. "Is it true?" I asked.

Mom looked a little **bugged**. Suddenly, I got **butterflies in my stomach**. Maybe Krista was just making it all up. "That **snake in the grass**," mumbled Mom.

"What?" I asked puzzled.

"Krista," she said. "I told her to keep it a secret! She's **in the doghouse** for sure!"

"Then it's true!" I said. "When can I have it? Whom can I invite? What will we have to eat? How…"

"Whoa," said Mom. "**Hold your horses**, Jeannie. Your birthday isn't for three weeks."

"Did Dad say OK already?" I asked.

"Yes, as long as you girls promise **no monkey business** and cut the noise by 10 o'clock."

I put my finger to my lips. "You won't **hear a peep** out of us!" I whispered.

"Well, I guess the pajama party is on then."

"YIPPEE!" I yelled. Then I said, "Whoops. I mean *yippee*," in my very quiet voice.

Read or listen to the story again. Then answer these questions about the idioms. To help you find them, the idioms are in **dark print** in the story.

1. To what animal do you think *bright-eyed and bushy-tailed* refers? _____

2. If you are *bright-eyed and bushy-tailed*, how are you feeling? _____

3. When Krista *let the cat out of the bag*, what did she really do? _____

   _____

4. What kind of things do you think Mom might consider *monkey business*? _____

   _____

5. What expression means to be sneaky? _____

6. Describe a time you had *butterflies in your stomach*. _____

Name _____   Date _____

Idiom ▶ **let the cat out of the bag**

Meaning ▶ **to tell or give away a secret**

How It Is Used ▶ Ricky overheard his parents talking about taking the family to a giant water park for a day of fun in the sun. He was so excited that he **let the cat out of the bag** and told his brother what he heard.

Which Is Right? ▶ Read the two selections. Choose the one in which **let the cat out of the bag** is used as an idiom. Circle the number of your choice.

❶ Jodi heard something moving in her closet. When she went to investigate, she saw that her cat, Mort, had crawled inside her laundry bag. Jodi laughed, and then *let the cat out of the bag*.

❷ Taylor's mother often came to school to help out. One day he heard his teacher and his mom planning a class party. When Cheryl said that she wondered if the class was going to have a holiday party, Taylor *let the cat out of the bag*.

Idiom ▶ **clam up**

Meaning ▶ **stop talking; keep quiet; refuse to speak**

How It Is Used ▶ When Karla's dad walked into her room past her bedtime, he saw she was on the phone, laughing and talking. "**Clam up** and go to sleep!" he said sternly.

Which Is Right? ▶ Read the two selections. Choose the one in which **clam up** is used as an idiom. Circle the number of your choice.

❶ The old fisherman went out on his boat everyday. Although he was fishing for lobster, every so often, he would pull a *clam up* in his net.

❷ The people boarded the boat with high hopes of spotting a whale. As they trolled out to sea, they chattered among themselves. Suddenly, the captain announced: "This is a whale-watching trip. If you want to see a whale, you will all have to *clam up* and watch!"

Name _____ Date _____

Idiom ▶ **bright-eyed and bushy-tailed**

Meaning ▶ **wide-awake, lively, and alert**

How It Is Used ▶ Dennis had always dreamed of being able to play the guitar. When his mom signed him up for lessons, Dennis was thrilled. Although his lessons didn't begin until 5 o'clock, Dennis was there and waiting at 4:45, **bright-eyed and bushy-tailed**.

Which Is Right? ▶ Read the two selections. Choose the one in which **bright-eyed and bushy-tailed** is used as an idiom. Circle the number of your choice.

❶ Dad usually sleeps late on Saturdays. But this Saturday, early in the morning, he was awakened by leaves rustling in the tree outside. Dad got up to have a look. There, right outside the window, staring back at him was a big squirrel, *bright-eyed and bushy-tailed*.

❷ Mom was excited when she got the job she wanted at a bank. Now, every morning she is up early, all *bright-eyed and bushy-tailed*.

Idiom ▶ **bugged/bug off**

Meaning ▶ **annoyed; bothered/leave; go away; stop annoying**

How It Is Used ▶ I am really **bugged** by people who claim to be your friend only when they want something. But then, when you just want to hang out, they want you to **bug off**.

Which Is Right? ▶ Read the two selections. Choose the one in which **bug off** is used as an idiom. Circle the number of your choice.

❶ My older brother likes to work on cars. When nobody else is around, he shows me stuff and lets me help. But, if any of his friends come by, he tells me to *bug off*!

❷ Uncle Jack is always cleaning his truck. He washes, waxes, and polishes it every weekend. Once I saw him take 20 minutes just to get a *bug off* his windshield.

#50158—*Idioms and Other English Expressions* © Shell Education

Name _____   Date _____

Idiom ▶	**butterflies in one's stomach**
Meaning ▶	**nervous or excited about something about to happen**
How It Is Used ▶	I didn't mind writing my report about bears, but thinking about reading it in front of the class gives me **butterflies in my stomach**.
Which Is Right? ▶	Read the two selections. Choose the one in which **butterflies in one's stomach** is used as an idiom. Circle the number of your choice.

❶ Do you know why little kids have to be watched all the time? It's because they try things that they shouldn't because they don't know any better. For example, when I was two, I got sick and had to have my stomach pumped. They found dirt, a leaf, four worms, and two *butterflies in my stomach*!

❷ My family came to the United States when I was just a baby. I never knew my grandparents, so when they arrived for a visit, I had *butterflies in my stomach*.

Idiom ▶	**snake in the grass**
Meaning ▶	**an untrustworthy, sneaky, or deceitful person**
How It Is Used ▶	Shannon thought Kelly was her friend. But when Shannon told Kelly a secret, Kelly went behind her back and told everybody. "She's no friend," said Shannon, "She is a **snake in the grass**."
Which Is Right? ▶	Read the two selections. Choose the one in which **snake in the grass** is used as an idiom. Circle the number of your choice.

❶ Carlos looked up to his cousin, Alberto, but Alberto could be a real *snake in the grass*. One time Alberto tricked Carlos into spending all day looking for his lost key by offering him a reward. When Carlos found the key, Alberto said, "Here's your reward." He then patted Carlos on the back and said, "Thanks, kid."

❷ One time, Carlos was at his cousin Alberto's house. Alberto was playing catch with his friends out in the field. Carlos shouted, "Hey Alberto, you had better be careful. The other day I saw a *snake in the grass* right where you are."

Name _____ Date _____

Idiom ▶ **in the doghouse**

Meaning ▶ **in trouble for something; in disgrace or shame**

How It Is Used ▶ Paula promised to call home when she arrived at her friend Soyun's house. The girls got there at 4 o'clock, but Paula forgot to call home. At 5:30, she remembered and said to Soyun, "I'm **in the doghouse**, for sure!" as she dialed the number.

Which Is Right? ▶ Read the two selections. Choose the one in which **in the doghouse** is used as an idiom. Circle the number of your choice.

❶ On Friday, Frankie's mom got home early and parked her car in the garage. Frankie tried to push his bike through, but scraped the paint on the side of his mom's car. "Uh, oh," he said to himself. "I am going to be *in the doghouse* for this."

❷ It was a hot day. Ben's dog, Sonny, could usually be found sleeping in the shade of the big tree out front. But, when Ben got home, Sonny was nowhere to be found. Ben ran into the house shouting, "Sonny's missing!" His sister did not even look up from her book. "He's *in the doghouse*," she said. "It's cooler in there."

Idiom ▶ **hold your horses**

Meaning ▶ **slow down; take your time; be patient**

How It Is Used ▶ Lynn saw her classmate with a pen that looked just like the one she had lost. Lynn promptly accused him of stealing her pen. "Whoa! **Hold your horses**, Lynn," said Mr. Kaplan. "Let's find out the facts before you accuse anyone of stealing."

Which Is Right? ▶ Read the two selections. Choose the one in which **hold your horses** is used as an idiom. Circle the number of your choice.

❶ The race horses had been training for months. When the men tried to walk the horses out to the track, they began to rear up and snort. "*Hold your horses*," the judge announced over the speaker. "Keep them calm until the race is ready to begin."

❷ At the park, we waited in line for an hour to ride the big roller coaster. As soon as we got off the two-minute ride, Chris began to run to get in line to go on again. "*Hold your horses*, Chris!" we shouted. "Maybe we should try another ride instead of waiting again for this one."

Name _____ Date _____

Idiom ▶ **monkey business**

Meaning ▶ **behaving in a silly or mischievous way**

How It Is Used ▶ Miss Nelson's students did not listen and were often noisy and disrespectful. Miss Nelson had finally had enough of their **monkey business**.

Which Is Right? ▶ Read the two selections. Choose the one in which **monkey business** is used as an idiom. Circle the number of your choice.

❶ One night at the zoo, a guard heard quite a commotion coming from the chimpanzee area. He went to investigate and found that the chimps were just playing and making noise as they often do. "Nothing to worry about," he muttered to himself. "Just monkeys doing *monkey business*."

❷ Mom walked into Lizzy's room to put away some laundry. Lizzy immediately hid something behind her back. "What are you hiding?" Lizzy's mom asked. "Nothing," giggled Lizzy. "Stop the *monkey business*, Lizzy, and show me what you are hiding," her mom demanded.

Idiom ▶ **hear a peep**

Meaning ▶ **hear even the smallest sound**

How It Is Used ▶ Jorge was almost asleep when Dad asked where his favorite CD was. Marie told him that Jorge had been playing it in his room. "I'll tiptoe in and get it," Marie said. "Don't worry, Jorge won't wake up. He won't **hear a peep** out of me."

Which Is Right? ▶ Read the two selections. Choose the one in which **hear a peep** is used as an idiom. Circle the number of your choice.

❶ Ed liked visiting his grandpa's farm. At night it was so still and quiet that you couldn't *hear a peep*.

❷ Ed went down to the barn early in the morning. The animals were pretty noisy, but Ed could *hear a peep* from a tiny chick that had wandered outside.

Idioms About Food

This unit highlights idioms based on food. Below are two lists of idioms that have something to do with food. The first, *Ten to Teach*, presents the 10 expressions introduced and taught in this unit. The second, *More to Mention*, offers additional expressions in this theme that you may want to mention or use to create additional activities.

Ten to Teach

1. piece of cake
2. chew out/get chewed out
3. have a sweet tooth
4. doesn't grow on trees
5. going bananas

6. take with a grain of salt
7. butter someone up
8. in a nutshell
9. food for thought
10. eat one's words

More to Mention

▶ takes the cake

▶ hot potato

▶ bowl of cherries

▶ feel one's oats

▶ walking on eggshells

▶ bite off more than one can chew

▶ couch potato

▶ apple of my eye

▶ just desserts

▶ proof is in the pudding

▶ out to lunch

Using This Unit

Begin by reading to students the basic *Ten to Teach* idioms. First, ask students if they have ever heard or used any of these expressions, and if so, how and where. Next, tell the students that you are going to read the expressions again, and this time they are to listen for anything they have in common. Accept all answers, and then point out that all the expressions refer in some way to food. Teach or review the definition of an idiom—an expression that means something other than what the words actually say. If you like, read the list a third time and let students speculate on what each idiom might really mean.

On the next page is a story that includes the *Ten to Teach* idioms. Note that the story is not intended to be an example of good writing; it would not be natural to use 10 idioms in such a short piece. The purpose of the story is simply to use all the expressions in context. The story is at approximately a 2.8 reading level. Use this information to read it aloud to students, have them read it, or both. This reproducible page includes the story and questions for students to answer related to the idioms used.

The final five pages of the unit introduce the basic *Ten to Teach* idioms individually, two to a page. These can be reproduced as is, or cut apart into separate cards. Use these after the story to reinforce the meanings of the idioms or test students' understanding of them. Or, use them before the story as preparation for reading or for scaffolding as needed.

Optional: Use one of the ideas or activities in the introductory section of this book as an extension or follow-up to the unit.

Name _____ Date _____

Below is a letter that includes 10 idioms related to food. Can you tell what they mean?

Dear Ronnie,

You know how we saved up our allowance to go to Splash Park, but then we found out that the price went up? So, as planned, I asked my mom for a raise in my allowance. I thought it would be a **piece of cake**. But mom asked me what I was doing with the allowance I was already getting. Before I could answer, she kept complaining about how I'm always asking for money. I will never understand why parents **chew you out** by asking questions and not giving you a chance to answer. "What do you do? Spend it all on candy? I know you **have a sweet tooth**, but money **doesn't grow on trees**! You need to be more responsible!" she yelled.

Just then Dad walked in. He saw that Mom was **going bananas**, but Dad takes Mom's temper **with a grain of salt**. "Hold on, honey," he said. He always calls her "honey" when he wants to **butter her up**.

"I understand why you think a raise in allowance is not reasonable. But we were just talking about how the cost of living keeps going up. That's true for kids as well as parents. Don't you think kids should get a cost of living raise as well? It's at least **food for thought**," Dad said.

Dad smiled at me, knowingly. Sure enough, Mom calmed down and agreed to raise my allowance. Dad sure made her **eat her words**! So, **in a nutshell**, I will able to save enough in a couple of weeks to go to Splash Park.   How did you do with your parents?

Your friend,

Michael

Read or listen to the letter again. Then answer these questions about the idioms. To help you find them, the idioms are in **dark print** in the story.

1. Did Michael think it would be easy to get a raise in his allowance? How do you know? _____

2. What kind of foods would someone with a *sweet tooth* like to eat? _____

_____

3. Did Dad take Mom's temper seriously or not? _____

4. Is it good or bad to be *chewed out*? _____

5. Explain in your own words what *made her eat her words* really means. _____

_____

Name _____ **Date** _____

Idiom ▶ **piece of cake**

Meaning ▶ **a task that is easily accomplished**

How It Is Used ▶ Joey thought it would be difficult to learn how to rollerblade. But the first time he put on skates, he discovered it was easier than he thought. "This is a **piece of cake**," he said to his brother.

Which Is Right? ▶ Read the two selections. Choose the one in which **piece of cake** is used as an idiom. Circle the number of your choice.

❶ It was John's birthday, and his mom was busy baking a cake. His sister, Kate, walked into the kitchen, opened the pantry, and reached for a cookie. "No sweets for you," her mother said. "Don't you want to wait for a *piece of cake*?"

❷ Dan had never liked math, but everything seemed to make sense when his new teacher, Mrs. Malloy, explained it. "Math is my favorite subject this year," Dan told his mom when his report card arrived. "In fact, it's a *piece of cake*!"

Idiom ▶ **chew out/get chewed out**

Meaning ▶ **scold severely or angrily**

How It Is Used ▶ As I typed the final page of my report, I hoped that my uncle would not **chew me out** for using his computer without asking him first.

Which Is Right? ▶ Read the two selections. Choose the one in which **chew out/get chewed out** is used as an idiom. Circle the number of your choice.

❶ "It's fun to watch what goes on at the birdfeeder," my cousin said. "One woodpecker will actually squawk loudly to *chew out* another for taking his space at the feeder or water dish."

❷ Early in the morning, three deer came by our yard and *chewed out* all Mom's newly planted flowers. "I love deer," my mom sighed, "but I really don't like that they ate all my pretty plants."

Name _____ Date _____

Idiom ▶ **sweet tooth**

Meaning ▶ **a special liking for sweet, sugary foods**

How It Is Used ▶ Having a **sweet tooth** can make you want to eat more foods with fat and sugar than you should.

Which Is Right? ▶ Read the two selections. Choose the one in which **sweet tooth** is used as an idiom. Circle the number of your choice.

❶ Nate had to have a tooth pulled to make room for other teeth that were coming in. When the dentist showed him the large tooth that was removed, Nate quickly forgot about how nervous he had been and said, "Boy, what a *sweet tooth*! One this big should be worth some money from the Tooth Fairy."

❷ When the family arrived at the county fair, Mario noticed all the food stands. "Mmm, look at all the yummy treats!" he said. "Mom, may I have cotton candy, a caramel apple, and an ice cream cone while we're here? You know I have a *sweet tooth*!"

Idiom ▶ **doesn't grow on trees**

Meaning ▶ **is not plentiful or easily replaced; does not happen naturally**

How It Is Used ▶ Jordan wished he had a new bike. When he asked his father for one, dad answered, "Unfortunately, money **doesn't grow on trees**." Jordan then decided that he'd think of a way to earn some money on his own.

Which Is Right? ▶ Read the two selections. Choose the one in which **doesn't grow on trees** is used as an idiom. Circle the number of your choice.

❶ "What did you learn on your field trip to the cranberry bog?" mom asked. I proudly replied, "I learned that a cranberry *doesn't grow on trees* or shrubs like some other berries. It grows in a bog, which is a water-filled field or marsh."

❷ Aunt Cindy told me to save the birthday cash that she gave me. "Money *doesn't grow on trees*, you know," she reminded me. I knew she was right. Even though I wanted to spend it, in the end, I decided to save the money.

Idioms About Food *(cont.)*

Name _____ Date _____

Idiom ▶ **going bananas**

Meaning ▶ **becoming uncontrollably excited, angry, or silly**

How It Is Used ▶ The day of the play, Sarah was **going bananas** because she couldn't find her costume.

Which Is Right? ▶ Read the two selections. Choose the one in which **going bananas** is used as an idiom. Circle the number of your choice.

❶ "Stop *going bananas*," I scolded my sister. "Riding the city bus for the first time is no big deal."

❷ Mom and Grandma got ready to go shopping at a farmer's market. Where they were *going, bananas* and pineapples—Grandma's favorites—were especially good.

Idiom ▶ **take with a grain of salt**

Meaning ▶ **doubt; not fully believing or trusting something**

How It Is Used ▶ Kathy heard from a friend that her dog was found, but she decided she would take the news **with a grain of salt**. She had been disappointed before when it turned out that a dog that only looked like hers had been spotted.

Which Is Right? ▶ Read the two selections. Choose the one in which **take with a grain of salt** is used as an idiom. Circle the number of your choice.

❶ Grandpa was on a special diet and couldn't eat a lot of salt. He was having a hard time adjusting to eating his favorite foods a different way. "I just can't get used to corn on the cob only *taken with a grain of salt*," he complained.

❷ The forest ranger listened to the excited campers' report. "I know you think you saw a jackal near your tent last night, but I have to *take that with a grain of salt*," he stated. "It was probably just a coyote. Jackals live in Africa and Asia, not Arizona."

Name _____ Date _____

Idiom ▶ **butter someone up**

Meaning ▶ **flatter or try to get a favor by praising someone**

How It Is Used ▶ Cheryl really wanted to take dance lessons, but they were expensive. She made a pretty card for her mom to **butter her up** before asking her to pay for the lessons.

Which Is Right? ▶ Read the two selections. Choose the one in which **butter someone up** is used as an idiom. Circle the number of your choice.

❶ "Don't expect that you can *butter me up* each morning so I will braid your hair," I cautioned my sister. "You need to braid it yourself because I don't always have time to do it."

❷ When Jules saw dad taking fresh-baked biscuits from the oven, he exclaimed, "I just love your hot biscuits for breakfast! *Butter me up* a big one!"

Idiom ▶ **in a nutshell**

Meaning ▶ **to the point, briefly, or in just a few words**

How It Is Used ▶ The teacher ended the history lesson in one sentence, "**In a nutshell**, Amelia Earhart was never found."

Which Is Right? ▶ Read the two selections. Choose the one in which **in a nutshell** is used as an idiom. Circle the number of your choice.

❶ Abby is going to water the Browns's flowers while they are out of town. Mrs. Brown showed Abby around the yard and said, "Please don't forget to water the two potted plants on the deck and the four potted plants by the front door. *In a nutshell*, water six potted plants."

❷ The tour guide at the nature center told the group, "Squirrels eat nuts. They carry them in their cheeks back to their nests. They crack the nut and eat the soft nut found *in a nutshell*."

Name _____ Date _____

Idiom ▶ **food for thought**

Meaning ▶ **an idea worth thinking about or considering**

How It Is Used ▶ Marty and Dave were editing partners in class. "Thanks for the suggestion," Marty said after hearing Dave's comment. "It's good **food for thought**."

Which Is Right? ▶ Read the two selections. Choose the one in which **food for thought** is used as an idiom. Circle the number of your choice.

❶ "Should we make Aunt Judy a gift basket of brownies for Valentine's Day?" I asked my mom. "That is certainly *food for thought*," she replied. "Let's think about it."

❷ Linda had a diary that she called her special "thought book." She had extra blank books, too, and her brother, Andy, wanted some. He brought a plate of cookies to her room, offering to trade her the *food for thought* books.

Idiom ▶ **eat one's words**

Meaning ▶ **admit to being or saying something wrong**

How It Is Used ▶ When I told Uncle Bud that I was sure that horses could live to be 75 years old, he told me to look it up in the encyclopedia. "If that's not true, then you will have to **eat your words**," said Uncle Bud.

Which Is Right? ▶ Read the two selections. Choose the one in which **eat one's words** is used as an idiom. Circle the number of your choice.

❶ "Look. I made cookies in the shape of letters," Maya said. "Now I can spell C-A-T and other words with my cookies. Then I can *eat my words*."

❷ "I may have to *eat my words*," said Erin, "but I don't think Dan will win the race today."

Eye, Ear, and Nose Idioms

This unit highlights eye, ear, and nose idioms. Below are two lists of idioms about these facial features. The first, *Ten to Teach*, presents the 10 expressions introduced and taught in this unit. The second, *More to Mention*, offers additional expressions in this theme that you may want to mention or use to create additional activities.

Ten to Teach

1. eagle-eyed
2. keep one's eyes peeled
3. see eye to eye
4. fall upon deaf ears
5. didn't bat an eyelash

6. eyes in the back of one's head
7. put one's nose to the grindstone
8. nose around
9. plain as the nose on one's face
10. pulled the wool over one's eyes

More to Mention

► in one ear and out the other
► keep one's nose out

► right under one's nose
► lend an ear
► more than meets the eye

► keep one's nose clean
► take the red-eye
► follow your nose

Using This Unit

Begin by reading to students the basic *Ten to Teach* idioms. First ask students if they have ever heard or used any of these expressions, and if so, how and where. Next, tell the students that you are going to read the expressions again, and this time they are to listen for anything they have in common. Accept all answers, and then point out that all the expressions refer to features on a face. Teach or review the definition of an *idiom*—an expression that means something other than what the words actually say. If you like, read the list a third time and let students speculate on what each idiom might really mean.

On the next page is a story that includes the *Ten to Teach* idioms. Note that the story is not intended to be an example of good writing; it would not be natural to use 10 idioms in such a short piece. The purpose of the story is simply to use all the expressions in context. The story is at approximately a 2.8 reading level. Use this information to read it aloud to students, have them read it, or both. This reproducible page includes the story and questions for students to answer related to the idioms used.

The final five pages of the unit introduce the basic *Ten to Teach* idioms individually, two to a page. These can be reproduced as is, or cut apart into separate cards. Use these after the story to reinforce the meanings of the idioms or to test students' understanding of them. Or, use them before the story as preparation for reading or for scaffolding as needed.

Optional: Use one of the ideas or activities in the introductory section of this book as an extension or follow-up to the unit.

Name _____ Date _____

Below is a story that includes 10 eye, ear, and nose idioms. Can you tell what they mean?

Private Eye

My name is Evan, and when I grow up I want to be a detective. That takes a lot of skill and practice, so I decided to start right away. I put up a sign by our mailbox: *Lost something? Hire **Eagle-Eyed** Evan to find it!*

At first I had no business. Then, one day there was a note in the mailbox. It said: "I need help finding my lost wrench. I **keep my eyes peeled** for it, but still I can't seem to find it. I would like to hire Eagle-Eyed Evan to locate it for me."

It was from my neighbor, Max. He is an older man who spends a lot of time working in his garage and is always losing stuff.

At dinner, I told my family that I was getting my first private-eye job. My two sisters, who never **see eye to eye** on anything, were busy yakking. My announcement **fell upon deaf ears**. No matter. I had a job to do. So, I crossed the yard to Max's. He was in his garage as usual.

"I hear you need a private eye," I said bravely. "It will cost one dollar up front and another when I find it." Max **didn't bat an eyelash**. "Fine," he said. "Maybe you have **eyes in the back of your head**, but I don't—at least not any more. So, **put your nose to the grindstone** and find my wrench." He handed me a dollar.

I began to **nose around**. It didn't take long. The wrench was there by his workbench, **plain as the nose on my face**. I asked Max, "Is this the one?"

"Why, yes it is!" he said as he handed me another dollar.

On my way home I thought to myself, "That was too easy. I wonder if Max just **pulled the wool over my eyes**. I guess I will never know for sure."

Read or listen to the story again. Then answer these questions about the idioms. To help you find them, the idioms are in **dark print** in the story.

1. Do you think eagles have good eyesight? _____

2. Do the writer's sisters agree or disagree about most things? _____

3. How do you think the writer felt when his announcement fell upon deaf ears? __

   _____

4. Which idiom means *in plain sight*? _____

5. Would you want someone to *pull the wool over your eyes*? _____

   Why or why not?_____

Name _____ Date _____

Idiom ▶ **eagle-eyed**

Meaning ▶ **having excellent sight; able to see things that others miss**

How It Is Used ▶ Miss Swanson gave the class her usual **eagle-eyed** look during the spelling test. Later at recess I told my friend, "Miss Swanson never misses a thing."

Which Is Right? ▶ Read the two selections. Choose the one in which **eagle-eyed** is used as an idiom. Circle the number of your choice.

❶ Mrs. Ritter talked to me before I babysat for her son, Marcus. "Be sure you are really *eagle-eyed* when he is awake," she cautioned. "Two-year-olds can get into things really fast."

❷ Alison stared at the bald eagle at the zoo. She noticed it staring back at her, too. When her dad walked over, she said, "I've been *eagle-eyed*."

Idiom ▶ **keep one's eyes peeled**

Meaning ▶ **staying alert and watchful**

How It Is Used ▶ "**Keep your eyes peeled** for that mouse in the garage," said Gus. "He is pretty fast and hard to spot."

Which Is Right? ▶ Read the two selections. Choose the one in which keep one's **eyes peeled** is used as an idiom. Circle the number of your choice.

❶ On the way to Bass Lake, Uncle Jake told us, "*Keep your eyes peeled* for the turnoff to the lake."

❷ Dad stood at the sink peeling potatoes for dinner. He said, "The little buds on the potatoes are called eyes. This special tool helps me *keep the eyes peeled* off, as well as the skin. Then the potato can be cut up and used for soup or stew."

Name _____ Date _____

Idiom ▶ **see eye to eye**

Meaning ▶ **to agree or have the same opinion about something**

How It Is Used ▶ Maddie's dad said, "I am sorry, Maddie. We just don't see **eye to eye** about how much time you can spend watching TV."

Which Is Right? ▶ Read the two selections. Choose the one in which **see eye to eye** is used as an idiom. Circle the number of your choice.

❶ Boy, was I surprised when I opened the patio umbrella this morning. As I stuck my head up under the umbrella to find the hand crank, I discovered I was *seeing eye to eye* with a sleeping bat.

❷ My brother and I do not *see eye to eye* about what to give my mom for Mother's Day. I guess we will have to ask our dad for ideas.

Idiom ▶ **fall upon deaf ears**

Meaning ▶ **be ignored; not be heard**

How It Is Used ▶ The nurse's advice to the student to keep the bandage on his cut **fell upon deaf ears**. He took it off as soon as he got home.

Which Is Right? ▶ Read the two selections. Choose the one in which **fall upon deaf ears** is used as an idiom. Circle the number of your choice.

❶ Mom warned Tommy about having too many sugary drinks. However, her warning *fell upon deaf ears* and at his next visit to the dentist, Tommy had four cavities.

❷ Kayla's little brother is deaf in his right ear. Yesterday he fell off his tricycle. He wasn't seriously hurt, but he *fell upon his deaf ear* and skinned his jaw.

Name _____ Date _____

Idiom ▶ **didn't bat an eyelash**

Meaning ▶ **paid no attention; not affected, influenced, or surprised**

How It Is Used ▶ My flute teacher **didn't bat an eyelash** when I missed just one note of the song.

Which Is Right? ▶ Read the two selections. Choose the one in which **didn't bat an eyelash** is used as an idiom. Circle the number of your choice.

❶ James was riding his bike fast down the street. A tiny bug flew into his eye, but he didn't feel it. In fact, it was such a little bug that he *didn't bat an eyelash*.

❷ Susan *didn't bat an eyelash* when I told her that her cat refused to eat turkey. "He only likes fish," she flatly replied.

Idiom ▶ **eyes in the back of one's head**

Meaning ▶ **being aware of what is going on without seeing it directly**

How It Is Used ▶ In my house we can't get away with anything. It is almost as if my mom has **eyes in the back of her head**.

Which Is Right? ▶ Read the two selections. Choose the one in which eyes in the back of one's head is used as an idiom. Circle the number of your choice.

❶ After my sister put makeup on her *eyes, in the back of her head* she tied a pretty bow in her hair.

❷ When dad got home from the store, he told us what happened. "Candace warned me that a car was coming up fast behind us. She must have *eyes in the back of her head* because she was in the back seat reading her library book. She may have helped me avoid an accident!"

Name _____ Date _____

Idiom ▶ **put one's nose to the grindstone**

Meaning ▶ **to make a serious effort; to work hard**

How It Is Used ▶ Mark had to put his **nose to the grindstone** to get an *A* on his science test.

Which Is Right? ▶ Read the two selections. Choose the one in which **put one's nose to the grindstone** is used as an idiom. Circle the number of your choice.

❶ After my grandpa sharpened his tools, I *put my nose to the grindstone*. You could smell a strong metal odor coming from his sharpening stone.

❷ Mom warned me that I would have to really *put my nose to the grindstone* if I wanted to win a ribbon in the science fair.

Idiom ▶ **nose around**

Meaning ▶ **to investigate or examine**

How It Is Used ▶ Dad was busy working at the computer when I came in to get something. "I haven't seen your little sister all morning," he said. "Would you go **nose around** and see what she is up to?"

Which Is Right? ▶ Read the two selections. Choose the one in which **nose around** is used as an idiom. Circle the number of your choice.

❶ The doctor asked why I came to see him today. I explained that for the last three days I'd had a rash on my *nose, around* my eyes, and on my forehead.

❷ Melinda heard a strange noise in the garage. She decided to *nose around* to see what it might be. It turned out that a bird had gotten trapped in the garage, so she opened the door for him to fly out.

Name _____ Date _____

Idiom ▶ **plain as the nose on one's face**

Meaning ▶ **clearly visible; without a doubt**

How It Is Used ▶ My sister asked me to help her look for her keys. But as soon as I walked into her room, there they were on her dresser, **plain as the nose on my face**.

Which Is Right? ▶ Read the two selections. Choose the one in which **plain as the nose on one's face** is used as an idiom. Circle the number of your choice.

❶ I watched as Valerie struggled to get on the horse. Once on, she had trouble getting her foot in the stirrup and dropped the reins. It was as *plain as the nose on my face* that Valerie did not have much experience riding a horse.

❷ People were staring at me. The reason was *plain, as the nose on my face* looked like a big red apple due to a bee sting.

Idiom ▶ **pull the wool over one's eyes**

Meaning ▶ **to fool, trick, or deceive someone**

How It Is Used ▶ Dad knew how much the car was worth. The salesman wanted my dad to buy the car. The salesman tried **to pull the wool over his eyes** by saying that it was worth more than it really was.

Which Is Right? ▶ Read the two selections. Choose the one in which **pull the wool over one's eyes** is used as an idiom. Circle the number of your choice.

❶ My friend tried to *pull the wool over my eyes*. She said that she had forgotten my birthday, but she really had a present hidden behind her back.

❷ When I went to the movies, I wore the wool cap my grandma knitted for me. Good thing, too, because during the scary parts, I would *pull the wool over my eyes*.

Action Idioms

This unit highlights idioms that describe actions. Below are two lists of idioms that begin with verbs, or action words. The first, *Ten to Teach*, presents the 10 expressions introduced and taught in this unit. The second, *More to Mention*, offers additional expressions in this theme that you may want to mention or use to create additional activities.

Ten to Teach

1. blow the whistle
2. rock the boat
3. bite one's tongue
4. get off the hook
5. draw the line

6. hit the nail on the head
7. carry the ball
8. get to the bottom of
9. chill out
10. catch you later

More to Mention

▶ beat around the bush
▶ bury the hatchet
▶ come out of one's shell
▶ burn one's bridges

▶ put a cork in it
▶ hold your horses
▶ saw logs
▶ throw in the towel

▶ kick the bucket
▶ pull oneself together

Using This Unit

Begin by reading to students the basic *Ten to Teach* idioms. First, ask students if they have ever heard or used any of these expressions, and if so, how and where. Next, tell the students that you are going to read the expressions again, and this time they are to listen for anything they have in common. Accept all answers, and then point out that all the expressions begin with verbs, or action words. Teach or review the definition of an *idiom*—an expression that means something other than what the words actually say. If you like, read the list a third time and let students speculate on what each idiom might really mean.

On the next page is a story that includes the *Ten to Teach* idioms. Note that the story is not intended to be an example of good writing; it would not be natural to use 10 idioms in such a short piece. The story is written at about a 1.0 reading level. The purpose of the story is simply to use all the expressions in context. The story is a phone conversation, which demonstrates how frequently people use idioms in casual conversation. You may want to have two students read it as if on the phone. This reproducible page includes the story and questions for students to answer related to the idioms used.

The final five pages of the unit introduce the basic *Ten to Teach* idioms individually, two to a page. These can be reproduced as is, or cut apart into separate cards. Use these after the story to reinforce the meanings of the idioms or to test students' understanding of them. Or, use them before the story as preparation for reading or for scaffolding as needed.

Optional: Use one of the ideas or activities in the introductory section of this book as an extension or follow-up to the unit.

Name _____ Date _____

Below is a story that includes 10 idioms that begin with verbs. Can you tell what they mean?

Take Action: A Phone Conversation

Ring…

Joe: Hello?

Chris: Hey, Joe.

Joe: Hey. What's up?

Chris: Did you see what I saw during the test today?

Joe: Yeah, if you mean a certain person who looked like she was copying answers.

Chris: Should I **blow the whistle** on her or keep quiet and not **rock the boat**?

Joe: Well, if you **bite your tongue** about this, she will get away with it.

Chris: The trouble is that I am pretty sure, but not positive, that she was cheating.

Joe: If she was, do you want her to **get off the hook**?

Chris: No. I saw her do it before, but I let it pass. I guess it is time to **draw the line**.

Joe: You've **hit the nail on the head**. Now it is up to you to **carry the ball**.

Chris: I guess saying something is the only way to **get to the bottom of it**.

Joe: I know it will be hard, but try to **chill out**. Just do what you know is the right thing.

Chris: OK. I will. Thanks for helping me figure this out.

Joe: No problem. **Catch you later**.

Click

Read or listen to the conversation again. Then answer these questions about the idioms. To help you find them, the idioms are in **dark print** in the text.

1. If someone suggests that you **chill out**, circle the words that tell how you might be feeling.

   nervous   hot   scared   troubled   warm

   excited   anxious   feverish   worried

2. Joe and Chris are not talking about nails, balls, whistles, drawing lines, or catching each other. What are they talking about? Describe the problem and solution. _____

   _____

3. Would you *blow the whistle* or not *rock the boat*? _____

4. Is the language in this conversation more like or unlike the way you talk to a friend on the phone? How? _____

   _____

Name _____ Date _____

Idiom ▶ **blow the whistle**

Meaning ▶ **tattle; tell on someone who is doing something they shouldn't**

How It Is Used ▶ My brother Dave told Mom that he was going to his friend's house after school. I knew that they were really going to the mall. I wondered if I should **blow the whistle** on him.

Which Is Right? ▶ Read the two selections. Choose the one in which **blow the whistle** is used as an idiom. Circle the number of your choice.

❶ During testing time at school, we get a few minutes of extra recess. Mr. Martinez said that he would *blow the whistle* when it was time to line up.

❷ Our class took a field trip to the museum. The guide told us not to touch anything. She said that if we saw kids touching a display, we should *blow the whistle* on them.

Idiom ▶ **rock the boat**

Meaning ▶ **cause trouble where there wasn't any; upset a calm situation**

How It Is Used ▶ My parents were in a good mood last night. I decided not to **rock the boat** by asking if I could have a raise in my allowance.

Which Is Right? ▶ Read the two selections. Choose the one in which **rock the boat** is used as an idiom. Circle the number of your choice.

❶ Last summer, Tanya's family went to the lake for a week. The first day they rented a small boat. Tanya was nervous as she got in. She tried not to *rock the boat* as she stepped aboard.

❷ My sister and I argue a lot, but recently we have been getting along better. When she got a new sweater, I was tempted to ask her if I could borrow it, but I decided not to *rock the boat*.

Name _____ Date _____

Idiom ▶ **bite one's tongue**

Meaning ▶ **keep quiet; keep from giving one's opinion**

How It Is Used ▶ My seven-year-old sister decided to try a new hairstyle. It looked awful, but I decided to **bite my tongue** about it.

Which Is Right? ▶ Read the two selections. Choose the one in which **bite one's tongue** is used as an idiom. Circle the number of your choice.

❶ My Aunt Carol just had a baby. At breakfast my mom said, "Jaime, I can't wait until this weekend when we can all go to Aunt Carol's and meet the new baby. Won't that be fun?" I didn't really think so, but I knew it was a good time to *bite my tongue.*

❷ The dentist gave me a shot that made my mouth numb. He said it would wear off in a while, but that in the meantime I should be careful not to *bite my tongue.*

Idiom ▶ **get off the hook**

Meaning ▶ **get free from a bad situation or from facing punishment**

How It Is Used ▶ Kenny found an old library book under his bed. It was due a month ago. He knew he had to return it, but he hoped he would **get off the hook** from having to pay a fine.

Which Is Right? ▶ Read the two selections. Choose the one in which **get off the hook** is used as an idiom. Circle the number of your choice.

❶ Whenever Grandpa Joe visits, he tells us fishing stories. This time he said that he caught a fish that weighed 100 pounds. As usual, he didn't have any pictures. He says that all the big ones *get off the hook* before he can snap a picture.

❷ Jenna said that she would watch little Ben while mom went to the store. While Jenna was doing her homework, Ben knocked a lamp off the table and it broke into pieces on the floor. Jenna knew she'd never *get off the hook* for doing a poor job of watching Ben.

Name _____ Date _____

Idiom ▶ **draw the line**

Meaning ▶ **set a limit; decide that one has had enough of something**

How It Is Used ▶ My parents think that kids having cell phones is a good idea. That way kids can call if they ever need help. However, my parents **draw the line** at using the phone just to talk with friends.

Which Is Right? ▶ Read the two selections. Choose the one in which **draw the line** is used as an idiom. Circle the number of your choice.

❶ Work crews were repaving the street where Katelyn lives. She thought it was amazing how they were able to *draw the line* so straight down the middle of the street.

❷ My teacher, Mrs. Simmons, wants us to discuss things in class with partners. However, she *draws the line* when we talk about things other than the assignment.

Idiom ▶ **hit the nail on the head**

Meaning ▶ **be exactly right or guess correctly**

How It Is Used ▶ Sharon said to her friend, Jessica, "You'll never guess what I got you for your birthday!" Sharon was surprised when Jessica guessed and **hit the nail on the head**.

Which Is Right? ▶ Read the two selections. Choose the one in which **hit the nail on the head** is used as an idiom. Circle the number of your choice.

❶ There was a board coming loose in Grandma's kitchen. Kurt got a hammer out of the toolbox. Grandma said, "Be careful not to hit your fingers. Be sure that you *hit the nail on the head*."

❷ Mom is usually tired after work. One night she was singing as she made dinner. As I set the table I said, "Why are you so happy? Did you get a raise or something?" Mom smiled and said, "You *hit the nail on the head*. I was going to announce it during dinner."

 #50158—Idioms and Other English Expressions

Name _____ Date _____

Idiom ▶ **carry the ball**

Meaning ▶ **take control and continue on with something started**

How It Is Used ▶ Freddie has a paper route and has to deliver newspapers early every morning. When he broke his leg in a soccer game, his brother Len offered to **carry the ball** until Freddie could do it again.

Which Is Right? ▶ Read the two selections. Choose the one in which **carry the ball** is used as an idiom. Circle the number of your choice.

❶ Four students were working together on a social studies project. They chose Mike to be the group leader. They agreed that if Mike was absent, Dianne would *carry the ball*.

❷ Phil was on the freshman football team, but he just sat on the bench. Even though he never got to *carry the ball*, Phil's family went to every game to cheer on the team.

Idiom ▶ **get to the bottom of**

Meaning ▶ **find the true answer or solution to a question or mystery**

How It Is Used ▶ Lynnette's favorite jacket was missing. She suspected that one of her sisters borrowed it. She was determined to **get to the bottom of** what happened to the jacket.

Which Is Right? ▶ Read the two selections. Choose the one in which **get to the bottom of** is used as an idiom. Circle the number of your choice.

❶ At the hotel pool, Bobby asked Mark if he wanted to play a game. "We'll take turns throwing a nickel into the pool and the person who *gets to the bottom of* the pool first to pick it up, wins," Mark said.

❷ Dad was looking all over the house for his running shoes. He found one, but not the other. He wanted to *get to the bottom of* the mystery of the missing shoe. Just then our dog, Rusty, walked in carrying the missing shoe in his mouth!

Name _____ Date _____

Idiom ▶ **chill out**

Meaning ▶ **be calm, relaxed; don't worry**

How It Is Used ▶ Donna and Sharon were studying together for a big spelling test. "I am never going to be able to remember all these words!" said Donna. "**Chill out**," said Sharon. "You already know most of them. You'll do fine if we go over them one more time."

Which Is Right? ▶ Read the two selections. Choose the one in which **chill out** is used as an idiom. Circle the number of your choice.

❶ The snow looked pretty as it fell while we were all warm and cozy inside. Later, though, when I had to walk the dog, I got a *chill out* in the cold snowy air.

❷ Jimmy went to clean Acorn's cage and discovered that his pet snake was gone! He raced to his sister and asked her to help him search for Acorn. "*Chill out*," said his sister. "Here he is—curled around the bottom of my lamp!"

Idiom ▶ **catch you later**

Meaning ▶ **intend to talk with you or see you at a future time**

How It Is Used ▶ Dominic and his dad were getting a few things in the grocery store when his dad spotted an old friend. They talked for a few minutes and exchanged phone numbers. "**Catch you later**, Tony, and you too, Dominic," the man said as he waved good-bye.

Which Is Right? ▶ Read the two selections. Choose the one in which **catch you later** is used as an idiom. Circle the number of your choice.

❶ Carla noticed the new girl at the bus stop. She decided to ask her to sit with her on the bus. When they got off at school, Carla said, "Bye. I'll *catch you later*, OK?"

❷ The police arrived just as the robber left the store. Two officers began to chase him on foot, but he got away. "Don't think you are getting away," one officer said to himself as he stopped running. "We'll *catch you later*."

Idioms That Get or Keep

This unit highlights idioms that begin with *get* and *keep*. Below are two lists of idioms that do this. The first, *Ten to Teach*, presents the 10 expressions introduced and taught in this unit. The second, *More to Mention*, offers additional expressions in this theme that you may want to mention or use to create additional activities.

Ten to Teach

1. **get a kick out of**
2. **get under one's skin**
3. **get the runaround**
4. **get over it**
5. **get cold feet**

6. **keep it under wraps**
7. **keep one's cool**
8. **keep one's fingers crossed**
9. **keep the ball rolling**
10. **keep a straight face**

More to Mention

▶ get one's feet wet
▶ get the green light
▶ get you down

▶ get the show on the road
▶ get it off one's chest
▶ keep a lid on it

▶ keep on one's toes
▶ keep it to oneself
▶ keep a stiff upper lip

Using This Unit

Begin by reading to students the basic *Ten to Teach* idioms. First, ask students if they have ever heard or used any of these expressions, and if so, how and where. Next, tell the students that you are going to read the expressions again, and this time they are to listen for anything they have in common. Accept all answers, and then point out that all the expressions begin with *get* or *keep*. Teach or review the definition of an *idiom*—an expression that means something other than what the words actually say. If you like, read the list a third time and let students speculate on what each idiom might really mean.

On the next page is a story that includes the *Ten to Teach* idioms. Note that the story is not intended to be an example of good writing; it would not be natural to use 10 idioms in such a short piece. The story is written at about a 3.0 reading level. The purpose of the story is simply to use all the expressions in context. The story is a note from one friend to another, which clearly demonstrates how frequently people use idioms in casual communication. You may want to have one or two students read aloud to practice reading with appropriate expression. This reproducible page includes the story and questions for students to answer related to the idioms used.

The final five pages of the unit introduce the basic *Ten to Teach* idioms individually, two to a page. These can be reproduced as is, or cut apart into separate cards. Use these after the story to reinforce the meanings of the idioms or to test students' understanding of them. Or, use them before the story as preparation for reading or for scaffolding as needed.

Optional: Use one of the ideas or activities in the introductory section of this book as an extension or follow-up to the unit.

Name _____ Date _____

Below is a note that includes 10 idioms that begin with *get* or *keep*. Can you tell what they mean?

Hey Karina,

   You'll **get a kick out of** this, but you have got to **keep it under wraps**. You know how my sister **gets under my skin**, right? She's on the phone every night. I have asked her a million times to **keep a lid on it** and let someone else use the phone, but all I **get is the runaround**. "Just **get over it**!" is what she always says.

   It's hard to **keep your cool** around her sometimes. I thought going to my parents to complain would help. But they just smiled, as if that was a solution. I realized that if I wanted to ever use the phone, I'd have to take action myself. So I made a plan. "**Keep your fingers crossed** that this works," I said to myself as I walked up to her. She was on the phone, of course. She glared at me, but this was no time to **get cold feet**.

   "Uh, Stacey," I said. She just kept on talking. So I pointed above her head and said, "Uh, Stacey...."

   "What?" she barked. "Can't you see that I am on the phone?"

   "Yes," I said. I had to **keep the ball rolling**, so I continued, "but I wanted to let you know that a huge, hairy spider is on the wall just behind your head."

   Stacey screamed so loud that I am sure the person on the other end of the line screamed, too! She dropped the phone and ran squealing upstairs. It was hard to **keep a straight face**, but I picked up the phone and said, "Stacey will call you back later," and hung up. Finally, I got to use the phone! Pretty funny, huh?

                                                           Your friend,
                                                           Renee

---

Read or listen to the note again. Then answer these questions about the idioms. To help you find them, the idioms are in **dark print** in the text.

1. If you were asked to *keep something under wraps*, which of these would you do? Circle your answer.

    tell someone   keep it under your jacket   keep it a secret

2. On the back of this paper, write about a time when you couldn't keep a straight face.

3. Write each word next to the idiom that expresses it: *wish, annoys, enjoy, continue*

    a. keep the ball rolling: _____   b. get a kick out of: _____

    c. gets under my skin: _____   d. keep your fingers crossed: _____

Name _____ Date _____

Idiom ▶ **get a kick out of**

Meaning ▶ **enjoy; have fun when doing something; amused by**

How It Is Used ▶ Aaron was afraid that his birthday party would not be fun for his friends. But, when he saw that they were **getting a kick out of** the magician, he stopped worrying.

Which Is Right? ▶ Read the two selections. Choose the one in which **get a kick out of** is used as an idiom. Circle the number of your choice.

❶ Peter wanted to play soccer with the other kids, but he was afraid to try. He kept coming to practice, but it took over two weeks until the coach *got a kick out of* him. After that first one, he was no longer afraid.

❷ The school talent show was a huge success. When our teacher asked which performance we liked best, Sammy said, "I really *got a kick out of* Ann's juggling act."

Idiom ▶ **get under one's skin**

Meaning ▶ **annoy; bother; get someone upset or mad**

How It Is Used ▶ Tim was the last one picked for the dodge ball game—again. He couldn't understand why. "This really **gets under my skin**," he thought to himself.

Which Is Right? ▶ Read the two selections. Choose the one in which **gets under one's skin** is used as an idiom. Circle the number of your choice.

❶ Ellen saw the patch on her dad's arm. "How does that help you to quit smoking?" she asked. Dad answered, "There's something like medicine in the patch. It *gets under my skin* and helps me not want to smoke."

❷ I told my friends that I wouldn't let the classroom bully *get under my skin*. But when he made fun of me in front of the whole class, I couldn't help but get upset.

Name _____ Date _____

Idiom ▶ **get the runaround**

Meaning ▶ **told incomplete or incorrect information; delayed or misdirected**

How It Is Used ▶ Sally and her family made reservations for dinner so that they wouldn't have to wait. But when they arrived, their table wasn't ready. After 15 minutes, Sally's dad asked when they would be seated. He was told it would just be another minute. "I think we are **getting the runaround**," he said to the family.

Which Is Right? ▶ Read the two selections. Choose the one in which **get the runaround** is used as an idiom. Circle the number of your choice.

❶ At the baseball game, the coach whispered to the players, "When you *get the runaround* signal, it means to go ahead and try to steal third base."

❷ Scott and his mom went to the store to buy the new video game. First, they were told it was in aisle four and then they were told aisle eight. When they still couldn't find it, Scott's mom said, "I don't like to *get the runaround*."

Idiom ▶ **get over it**

Meaning ▶ **stop being bothered or upset by something that is over**

How It Is Used ▶ I really got upset when I studied for my math test and got a *B* instead of an *A*. I guess I just have to **get over it** and study harder next time!

Which Is Right? ▶ Read the two selections. Choose the one in which **get over it** is used as an idiom. Circle the number of your choice.

❶ I told Russ that I would win the obstacle race. "I have been practicing," I told him. "When I get to the wall, I will *get over it* faster than everyone else."

❷ On the final round of the spelling bee, Mary spelled her word wrong. Afterward, she could not seem to *get over it*. Her teacher said, "Let it go, Mary. Maybe you will get an easier word in next year's contest."

Name _____ Date _____

Idiom ▶ **get cold feet**

Meaning ▶ **become nervous or scared when something is about to happen**

How It Is Used ▶ For Halloween, Mr. Marshall decorates his house in a creepy way. Last year, he even hid in the bushes and jumped out at the kids. I hope this year I don't **get cold feet** when we go to his house to trick or treat.

Which Is Right? ▶ Read the two selections. Choose the one in which **get cold feet** is used as an idiom. Circle the number of your choice.

❶ Jodi practiced for months for her piano recital. She knew her music well, but was nervous about playing in front of people. As the day approached, she hoped she wouldn't *get cold feet.*

❷ When the third grade class was told they would go to the skating rink for their winter field trip, they were excited. However, some of them wondered if they would *get cold feet* after they skated on the ice for a couple of hours.

Idiom ▶ **keep it under wraps**

Meaning ▶ **keep something a secret or hidden**

How It Is Used ▶ My big sister is in a race against her best friend for sixth grade class president. The votes were counted on Friday, and the principal knows who won. However, he said he would **keep it under wraps** until Parents' Night next week.

Which Is Right? ▶ Read the two selections. Choose the one in which **keep it under wraps** is used as an idiom. Circle the number of your choice.

❶ During harvest season, farm growers keep oranges covered when there is cold weather. They know that if the orchard is in danger of being destroyed, they must *keep it under wraps* or risk losing the whole crop.

❷ Kyle's birthday is next week and his parents asked his brother what Kyle might like. Todd helped his parents pick out a new DVD he knows his brother wants, but he'll *keep it under wraps* until the big day.

Name _____ Date _____

Idiom ▶ **keep one's cool**

Meaning ▶ **be calm and not allow oneself to get excited or angry**

How It Is Used ▶ Larry was having trouble with a bully at school who teased and annoyed him. He wanted to do something mean back, but he decided to **keep his cool**. After all, two wrongs don't make a right!

Which Is Right? ▶ Read the two selections. Choose the one in which **keep one's cool** is used as an idiom. Circle the number of your choice.

❶ In the summer, my friend Jason always drinks lemonade. The last time Jason came over, I poured him a big glass of lemonade and added plenty of ice to help him *keep his cool*.

❷ Ben and his friend Matthew were riding bikes. Suddenly, Matthew heard Ben cry out. He had hit a rock and fell, and his knee was bleeding. Matthew remembered to *keep his cool* and followed the steps he learned in a first-aid class.

Idiom ▶ **keep one's fingers crossed**

Meaning ▶ **to have hope or wishful thinking**

How It Is Used ▶ Nick's favorite football team had made it to the Super Bowl. During the game, he **kept his fingers crossed** that they would win.

Which Is Right? ▶ Read the two selections. Choose the one in which **keep one's fingers crossed** is used as an idiom. Circle the number of your choice.

❶ My parents were downstairs discussing whether to go to the beach or to go camping for the yearly family trip. My brother *kept his fingers crossed* that our parents would decide on camping.

❷ Andy showed his friends a trick he could do—cross his first two fingers and his second two at the same time. Andy laughed and *kept his fingers crossed* as his friends tried to do it without any luck.

Name _____ Date _____

Idiom ▶ **keep the ball rolling**

Meaning ▶ **continue without stopping or delay**

How It Is Used ▶ At their yearly Halloween party, Lisa's parents had a haunted house, a tub of water to bob for apples, and some fun and scary games to **keep the ball rolling** during the evening.

Which Is Right? ▶ Read the two selections. Choose the one in which **keep the ball rolling** is used as an idiom. Circle the number of your choice.

❶ We went bowling for my seventh birthday party. My sister kept throwing her ball into the next lane. I didn't make any strikes, but at least I *kept the ball rolling*.

❷ Our math teacher challenged us with a game of solving problems in our heads, rather than using pencil and paper. It was pretty tough at first, but then it got fun. She *kept the ball rolling* by making each round of questions a little harder than the last.

Idiom ▶ **keep a straight face**

Meaning ▶ **keep from laughing, reacting, or showing expression on one's face**

How It Is Used ▶ At our house, the family likes to play card games, such as Go Fish. One of the things you have to do to play this game is **keep a straight** face so that no one can tell what cards you have.

Which Is Right? ▶ Read the two selections. Choose the one in which **keep a straight face** is used as an idiom. Circle the number of your choice.

❶ I like to draw. I especially like to design robots. I learned a long time ago that it is hard to draw and *keep a straight face* on a robot without using a ruler.

❷ My three-year-old brother gets mad whenever anyone laughs at him. So when he came into my room wearing one of my old nightgowns, I tried hard to *keep a straight face* and not crack up.

Idioms That Pull or Put

This unit highlights idioms that begin with *pull* and *put*. Below are two lists of idioms that do this. The first, *Ten to Teach*, presents the 10 expressions introduced and taught in this unit. The second, *More to Mention*, offers additional expressions in this theme that you may want to mention or use to create additional activities.

Ten to Teach

1. **pull a stunt**
2. **put one's foot in one's mouth**
3. **pull one's leg**
4. **put someone down**
5. **put in a good word**
6. **pull some strings**
7. **put one's money where one's mouth is**
8. **put one's finger on it**
9. **pull one in**
10. **put it/one to the test**

More to Mention

▶ pull a fast one
▶ pull it off
▶ pull the rug out from under
▶ pull up stakes
▶ pull the plug
▶ pull rank
▶ put one's best foot forward
▶ put one's foot down
▶ put the horse before the cart
▶ put all one's eggs in one basket

Using This Unit

Begin by reading to students the basic *Ten to Teach* idioms. First, ask students if they have ever heard or used any of these expressions, and if so, how and where. Next, tell the students that you are going to read the expressions again, and this time they are to listen for anything they have in common. Accept all answers, and then point out that all the expressions begin with *pull* or *put*. Teach or review the definition of an *idiom*—an expression that means something other than what the words actually say. If you like, read the list a third time and let students speculate on what each idiom might really mean.

On the next page is a poem that includes the *Ten to Teach* idioms. Note that the poem is not intended to be an example of good writing; it would not be natural to use 10 idioms in such a short piece. The story is written at about a 1.0 reading level. The purpose of the story is simply to use all the expressions in context. The poem demonstrates how frequently people use idioms in everyday language. You may want to have one or two students read aloud to practice reading with appropriate expression. This reproducible page includes the story and questions for students to answer related to the idioms used.

The final five pages of the unit introduce the basic *Ten to Teach* idioms individually, two to a page. These can be reproduced as is, or cut apart into separate cards. Use these after the story to reinforce the meanings of the idioms or to test students' understanding of them. Or, use them before the story as preparation for reading or for scaffolding as needed.

Optional: Use one of the ideas or activities in the introductory section of this book as an extension or follow-up to the unit.

Name _____ **Date** _____

Below is a poem that includes 10 idioms that begin with *pull* or *put*.   Can you tell what they mean?

My dad has a big brother.
His name is Drummin' Dave.
He's in an old guys' rock band
Which I think is pretty brave.

Say people of our parents' age
Can't **pull a stunt** like this?
You'll **put your foot in your mouth**
And take back every dis.
I wouldn't **pull your leg**,
They really rock the town.
If you came along to hear them
You wouldn't **put them down**.
I'll **put in a good word** for you.

I'll **pull some strings** and then,
Put my money where my mouth is—
You'll like them—bet you ten!

Can't **put my finger on it**.
There's somethin' 'bout these guys.
They go from dads and uncles
To cool before your eyes!

Their music really **pulls you in**.
They **put you to the test**.
You'll come away from their show
Thinkin' old guys are the best!

Read or listen to the poem again. Then answer these questions about the idioms. To help you find them, the idioms are in **dark print** in the text.

1. A "dis" is an expression that means the same as a *put-down*. What are you doing if you dis or put down someone? _____

   _____

2. If I am *pulling your leg*, am I kidding you or testing you? _____

3. If I *put my money where my mouth is*, am I feeling sure or unsure? _____

4. If I *pull some strings*, am I getting a favor or teasing? _____

5. If I can *put my finger on something*, do I know or not know what it is? _____

6. What ending was shortened in each of the following words from the poem: *drummin'*, *somethin'*, and *thinkin'*? _____

Idioms That Pull or Put *(cont.)*

Name _____ Date _____

Idiom ▶ **pull a stunt**

Meaning ▶ **to trick or deceive**

How It Is Used ▶ Jamal took his neighbor's three dogs for a walk. Then he walked over to Tammy's house and told her that he just got three new dogs. But she knew he was just trying to **pull a stunt** on her.

Which Is Right? ▶ Read the two selections. Choose the one in which **pull a stunt** is used as an idiom. Circle the number of your choice.

❶ Yesterday my family went to the circus. There were so many things going on at the same time. For example, as two clowns gave a big wagon full of dogs a *pull, a stunt* was being performed above them by an acrobat on the tightrope.

❷ I told my friend Erica about my plans to get someone else to do my homework that night. She warned, "If you *pull a stunt* like that, then you will be in trouble with both our teacher and your parents." When she put it like that, I decided not to go through with my plan and just do my homework.

Idiom ▶ **put one's foot in one's mouth**

Meaning ▶ **say the wrong thing or say something embarrassing**

How It Is Used ▶ You all need to be careful that you don't **put your foot in your mouth** when Sadie shows up with a black eye," the coach told the team. "We don't want to tease her about getting hit with the ball at last week's game."

Which Is Right? ▶ Read the two selections. Choose the one in which **put one's foot in one's mouth** is used as an idiom. Circle the number of your choice.

❶ My baby brother is just discovering that he has legs and feet. His new favorite game is to grab his leg and *put his foot in his mouth*.

❷ Laura felt so embarrassed. She told her mom that she didn't like her cousin's new outfit and her cousin overheard her from the next room. That made her cousin run outside, crying. "You really *put your foot in your mouth* this time," her mom said.

#50158—Idioms and Other English Expressions   © Shell Education

Name _____ Date _____

Idiom ▶ **pull one's leg**

Meaning ▶ **to say something untrue as a joke; to tease or fool someone**

How It Is Used ▶ My uncle Ben is full of jokes. He sure knows how to **pull your leg**, so his visits are always filled with fun and laughter.

Which Is Right? ▶ Read the two selections. Choose the one in which **pull one's leg** is used as an idiom. Circle the number of your choice.

❶ I noticed that my brand-new jeans looked like they had been worn, and I suspected my twin sister. "No *pulling my leg*," I said to her. "Did you wear my new jeans? I want an honest answer."

❷ Have you ever tried to *pull your leg* out of a tight pair of pants? It's almost impossible! Most of the time, you struggle to pull them off only to end up with the pants turned inside out.

Idiom ▶ **put someone down**

Meaning ▶ **to say something bad or negative about someone or something**

How It Is Used ▶ Someone who is constantly **putting me down** cannot be my friend. A good friend is someone who likes you and accepts the good and bad in you.

Which Is Right? ▶ Read the two selections. Choose the one in which **put someone down** is used as an idiom. Circle the number of your choice.

❶ I was giving the puppy a bath in the kitchen sink when I heard the doorbell ring. "Who is it?" I yelled. "I have a package for you," the deliveryman yelled back from the other side of the door. "I have my hands full right now!" I yelled back. "Please *put it down* on the doorstep."

❷ Kim was upset with one of her classmates, Jennifer. She overheard Jennifer *putting her down* in front of some of their friends. Jennifer's words made her feel hurt and angry.

Name _____ Date _____

Idiom ▶ **put in a good word**

Meaning ▶ **to say something in support or praise**

How It Is Used ▶ My brother wanted to earn some money, so I **put in a good word** about him to our neighbor. The following week, she called him to see if he would babysit for her son.

Which Is Right? ▶ Read the two selections. Choose the one in which **put in a good word** is used as an idiom. Circle the number of your choice.

❶ Mrs. Simms is Emma's neighbor. Sometimes Mrs. Simms needs a little help. Yesterday, Emma helped her move her garbage can to the curb. The next day, Mrs. Simms saw Emma's dad and *put in a good word* about her to him.

❷ My third-grade teacher is very talented and finds clever ways to teach us. For instance, she wrote a song for us called "*Put in a Good Word*." Her humorous song is about using colorful words when you write. What a terrific way to learn writing skills!

Idiom ▶ **pull some strings**

Meaning ▶ **use one's influence or power to get a favor**

How It Is Used ▶ Becky was disappointed that the store did not have the color of socks she needed for her costume. However, when the store clerk said she could **pull some strings** with the warehouse and get them to the store in a few days, Becky was happy.

Which Is Right? ▶ Read the two selections. Choose the one in which **pull some strings** is used as an idiom. Circle the number of your choice.

❶ Sometimes it really pays to have friends who know important people. My friend's dad *pulled some strings* with people he knew and got us half-price tickets for the water park.

❷ My baby brother got a handmade blanket for his first birthday. But my mom had to take it away after he *pulled some strings* on the edge and it started to fall apart.

Name _____ Date _____

Idiom	▶	**put one's money where one's mouth is**
Meaning	▶	**to be so certain that one would bet money on it**
How It Is Used	▶	Andy bet Sam that he would beat him in a game of checkers. Sam was confident he would win. "**Put your money where your mouth is**," Sam said.
Which Is Right?	▶	Read the two selections. Choose the one in which **put one's money where one's mouth is** is used as an idiom. Circle the number of your choice.

❶ "I'm going to score the winning goal at the game this Saturday," Jared told his team members. Eddie didn't like when Jared made predictions like that. "Why don't you *put your money where your mouth is*?" Eddie challenged him.

❷ My baby brother is always putting things in his mouth. We caught him once putting a quarter in his mouth, and my mom worries that one day he might swallow a coin and choke. So she told me to make sure not to *put my money where his mouth is*.

Idiom	▶	**put one's finger on it**
Meaning	▶	**to know or identify exactly; to point out precisely**
How It Is Used	▶	Maggie dreamed of having a collie. She couldn't quite **put her finger on** what she liked so much about that kind of breed, but collies had always seemed like the perfect pets.
Which Is Right?	▶	Read the two selections. Choose the one in which **put one's finger on it** is used as an idiom. Circle the number of your choice.

❶ I couldn't quite *put my finger on it*, but something was really wrong. A storm had moved in and the wind kept getting stronger and stronger. I turned on the TV and the newscaster said a small tornado was spotted in our county. He warned that we should stay inside.

❷ Checking out a book at the library is now so easy. With the help of a computer, I can do what is called a "self-check." All I have to do is swipe my library card, scan the book, find the button that says "checkout," and *put my finger on it*. All done!

Idioms That Pull or Put *(cont.)*

Name _____ Date _____

Idiom ▶ **pull one in**

Meaning ▶ **get your attention or get you involved in something**

How It Is Used ▶ Hopscotch is a very popular game that has been around for many years. You use chalk to draw the hopscotch pattern on a sidewalk or driveway. Players toss a marker onto one of the squares and try to hop over it. Like other games, it takes patience and practice to become good at it, but the game can really **pull you in**.

Which Is Right? ▶ Read the two selections. Choose the one in which **pull one in** is used as an idiom. Circle the number of your choice.

❶ On our trip to New York City, we stayed on the 32nd floor of a hotel. When we got to the room, we all rushed to the window to take in the view of the city. My brother exclaimed, "Wow! This view really *pulls you in*."

❷ My dad *pulled me in* the den and sat down with me. Together, we read the directions to put together the model car and things started to go better. I thought I could get by with only looking at the picture, but it was easy to see that I was wrong.

Idiom ▶ **put it/one to the test**

Meaning ▶ **to challenge something or someone**

How It Is Used ▶ After getting a new motor for the boat, Matthew took it out on the lake to **put it to the test**.

Which Is Right? ▶ Read the two selections. Choose the one in which **put it/one to the test** is used as an idiom. Circle the number of your choice.

❶ It had rained every day for weeks. As a result, everything was growing like crazy, including the lawn. Mowing the thick grass would surely *put my dad to the test*.

❷ To play the math game called "*Put It to the Test*," Daniel will need a special computer program.

This unit highlights idioms that are similes. Below are two lists of similes. The first, *Ten to Teach*, presents the 10 similes introduced and taught in this unit. The second, *More to Mention*, offers additional similes that you may want to mention or use to create additional activities.

Ten to Teach

1. **like two peas in a pod**
2. **as different as night and day**
3. **like a bump on a log**
4. **as quiet as a mouse**
5. **like a fish out of water**
6. **as easy as pie**
7. **as stiff as a board**
8. **feel like two cents**
9. **fit like a glove**
10. **like pulling teeth**

More to Mention

- ► eats like a horse/pig
- ► as cold as ice
- ► as hungry as a bear
- ► like music to one's ears
- ► as sweet as honey
- ► sings like a bird
- ► as green as grass
- ► as soft as silk
- ► fight like cats and dogs
- ► like water off a duck's back

Using This Unit

Begin by reading to students the basic *Ten to Teach* idioms. First, ask students if they have ever heard or used any of these expressions, and if so, how and where. Next, tell the students that you are going to read the expressions again, and this time they are to listen for anything they have in common. Accept all answers, and then point out that all the expressions compare one thing to another. Teach or review the definition of a *simile*—a comparison using *like* or *as*. If you like, read the list a third time and let students identify what the comparison is in each.

On the next page is a story that includes the *Ten to Teach* similes. Note that the story is not intended to be an example of good writing; it would not be natural to use 10 similes in such a short piece. The purpose of the story is simply to use all the expressions in context. The story is at approximately a 2.8 reading level. Use this information to read it aloud to students, have them read it, or both. This reproducible page includes the story and questions for students to answer related to the similes used.

The final five pages of the unit introduce the basic *Ten to Teach* similes individually, two to a page. These can be reproduced as is, or cut apart into separate cards. Note: Instead of identifying which example uses the phrase as an idiom, as in previous units in this book, now students are asked questions that lead them to decide if a phrase in a selection is used as a simile or not.

Optional: Use one of the ideas or activities in the introductory section of this book as an extension or follow-up to the unit.

Name _____ Date _____

Below is a story containing 10 similes. Can you tell what they are comparing?

> My brother and I are twins. Everyone says we are **like two peas in a pod**, but I think we are **as different as night and day**. I like to go out and do things. Paul just sits **like a bump on a log** in front of the TV, **as quiet as a mouse**.
>
> The other day, I got him to come outside and play kickball with us. I wanted him to **fit like a glove** on our team, but he was **like a fish out of water**. The ball is pretty big, so kicking it is **as easy as pie**. When Paul's turn came, he walked up **as stiff as a board** and actually missed the ball completely! I felt **like two cents** when our team lost. But, the guys let it roll off them **like water off a duck's back**.
>
> Later, at home, I told my mom that getting Paul to play was **like pulling teeth**! She said that he was just shy and that I should keep inviting him to play. In time, he would come around and might even be our best player. I guess she could be right. What do you think?

Read or listen to the story again. Then answer these questions about the similes. To help you find them, the similes are in **dark print** in the text.

1. Do you think *water rolls off a duck's back* easily? Why or why not? _____

   _____

2. What word in the expression *felt like two cents* tells you that it is a simile?

   _____

3. Underline the thing in the story that is being compared in each simile:

   a. *like pulling teeth*:   getting Paul to play   talking to Mom

   b. *as stiff as a board*:   Paul   how Paul walked

   c. *as easy as pie*:   kicking   getting Paul to play

4. Think of someone you know who you think is like you in some way and different in another way. Fill in the person's name and then finish this simile about the person.

   a. _____ and I are *like two peas in a pod* because

   _____

Name _____ Date _____

Simile ▶ **like two peas in a pod**

Meaning ▶ **alike in looks or behavior; identical; very close**

How It Is Used ▶ Maria had a cousin her age, but they had never met until they were eight years old. When they saw each other for the first time, they were amazed. They looked **like two peas in a pod**.

Recognizing Similes ▶ Remember: A simile is a comparison using *like* or *as*.

Read the selection. Answer the questions below.

Trying to get my little brother to eat vegetables is impossible. Mom says he'd probably starve before he would eat *two peas in a pod*.

❶ Is something being compared to something else? ◯ yes ◯ no

❷ Is the word *like* or *as* used to compare? ◯ yes ◯ no

❸ Are the words *two peas in a pod* part of a simile in this selection? ◯ yes ◯ no

---

Simile ▶ **as different as night and day**

Meaning ▶ **opposite**

How It Is Used ▶ My uncles are brothers, but you would never know it. One is very tall and has light hair and blue eyes. The other is short and has black hair and brown eyes. They look as different **as night and day**.

Recognizing Similes ▶ Remember: A simile is a comparison using *like* or *as*.

Read the selection. Answer the questions below.

Pepperoni! Mushroom! Onion! No onion! Ordering a pizza at our house is so hard because our tastes are *as different as night and day*.

❶ Is something being compared to something else? ◯ yes ◯ no

❷ Is the word *like* or *as* used to compare? ◯ yes ◯ no

❸ Are the words *different as night and day* part of a simile in this selection? ◯ yes ◯ no

---

Name _____ Date _____

Simile ▶ **like a bump on a log**

Meaning ▶ **unmoving; inactive; without response**

How It Is Used ▶ I don't like it when I get sick. I can't do anything except sit in bed. I'd rather go to school than just sit there **like a bump on a log**.

Recognizing Similes ▶ Remember: A simile is a comparison using *like* or *as*.

Read the selection. Answer the questions below.

Tyler was spending all his free time on the computer playing games. Yesterday his mom came in and said, "Tyler, how can you just sit in front of that screen *like a bump on a log*? Why don't you go out and get some fresh air?"

❶ Is something being compared to something else? ◯ yes ◯ no

❷ Is the word *like* or *as* used to compare? ◯ yes ◯ no

❸ Are the words *bump on a log* part of a simile in this selection? ◯ yes ◯ no

---

Simile ▶ **as quiet as a mouse**

Meaning ▶ **very quiet; without making noise**

How It Is Used ▶ We saw something move in the darkness across the campsite. My sister became **as quiet as a mouse**. I turned the flashlight on and saw a man coming toward us. "Are you kids OK?" the camp counselor asked. "I was just coming to check on everyone."

Recognizing Similes ▶ Remember: A simile is a comparison using *like* or *as*.

Read the selection. Answer the questions below.

We opened the door, hoping it would leave. We heard scratching, and then it became *quiet as a mouse* scrambled passed us and out the door.

❶ Is something being compared to something else? ◯ yes ◯ no

❷ Is the word *like* or *as* used to compare? ◯ yes ◯ no

❸ Are the words *quiet as a mouse* part of a simile in this example? ◯ yes ◯ no

---

Name _____   Date _____

Simile ▶	**like a fish out of water**
Meaning ▶	**out of place; not comfortable; awkward**
How It Is Used ▶	We took a trip to Mexico to visit my relatives. Of course, everyone there spoke Spanish. I was born in the United States and only speak English, so I felt **like a fish out of water**.
Recognizing Similes ▶	Remember: A simile is a comparison using *like* or *as*.

Read the selection. Answer the questions below.

When Cindy started at a new school, it seemed like everyone already knew one another and was part of a group. On her first day, she sat alone at lunch feeling *like a fish out of water*.

❶ Is something being compared to something else? ⭕ yes ⭕ no

❷ Is the word *like* or *as* used to compare? ⭕ yes ⭕ no

❸ Are the words *fish out of water* part of a simile in this example? ⭕ yes ⭕ no

---

Simile ▶	**as easy as pie**
Meaning ▶	**very easy; no problem; without difficulty**
How It Is Used ▶	George watched as Kevin did tricks on his skateboard. "Come on, George. Try it. It's **as easy as pie**." But George knew that if he tried one of the tricks, he would probably fall and get hurt.
Recognizing Similes ▶	Remember: A simile is a comparison using *like* or *as*.

Read the selection. Answer the questions below.

There were all sorts of goodies on the table for the school bake sale. Making the money they needed was *easy, as pie*, cakes, cookies, and cupcakes were sold one right after the other.

❶ Is something being compared to something else? ⭕ yes ⭕ no

❷ Is the word *like* or *as* used to compare? ⭕ yes ⭕ no

❸ Are the words *easy as pie* part of a simile in this example? ⭕ yes ⭕ no

---

Expressions That Are Similes (cont.)

Name _____ Date _____

Simile ▶	**as stiff as a board**	
Meaning ▶	**hard; rigid; unbendable**	
How It Is Used ▶	We waited in line for an hour to ride the Monster Roller Coaster. At first it didn't seem so high, but as Terry got closer, she became **as stiff as a board** with fear. At the last minute she decided to get out of line and just watch us ride.	
Recognizing Similes ▶	Remember: A simile is a comparison using *like* or *as*.	

Read the selection. Answer the questions below.

I left my bike out overnight last month. During the night it dropped below freezing, and the next day my seat and tires were as *stiff as a board*.

❶ Is something being compared to something else? ◯ yes ◯ no

❷ Is the word *like* or *as* used to compare? ◯ yes ◯ no

❸ Are the words *stiff as a board* part of a simile in this example? ◯ yes ◯ no

---

Simile ▶	**feel like two cents**	
Meaning ▶	**disgraced; embarrassed; shamed; worthless**	
How It Is Used ▶	Karen borrowed Kelly's sweater at recess. She still had it on when she went home. She threw it in her closet and forgot about it. Two weeks later, Kelly asked about her sweater and Karen **felt like two cents**.	
Recognizing Similes ▶	Remember: A simile is a comparison using *like* or *as*.	

Read the selection. Answer the questions below.

Ricky forgot his lunch. He *felt like two cents* when he had to ask his friend to borrow money to buy lunch.

❶ Is something being compared to something else? ◯ yes ◯ no

❷ Is the word *like* or *as* used to compare? ◯ yes ◯ no

❸ Are the words *feel like two cents* part of a simile in this example? ◯ yes ◯ no

---

#50158—Idioms and Other English Expressions

Name _____   Date _____

Simile ▶ **fit like a glove**

Meaning ▶ **fit perfectly; faultlessly**

How It Is Used ▶ Mom was trying on dresses all day, but she couldn't find one that she liked. Then she tried on the navy one, and it **fit like a glove**. Even the saleswoman told her she looked great in it.

Recognizing Similes ▶ Remember: A simile is a comparison using *like* or *as*.

Read the selection. Answer the questions below.

When it's really cold outside, I always wear my fur-lined gloves. They keep my hands warm and they look great. And no other gloves I've ever tried on have *fit me like those gloves* fit me.

❶ Is something being compared to something else? ◯ yes ◯ no

❷ Is the word *like* or *as* used to compare? ◯ yes ◯ no

❸ Are the words *fits like a glove* part of a simile in this example? ◯ yes ◯ no

---

Simile ▶ **like pulling teeth**

Meaning ▶ **very difficult**

How It Is Used ▶ My brother never wants to share. For example, there are two good TV shows on at the same time. Getting him to watch the one I like is **like pulling teeth**.

Recognizing Similes ▶ Remember: A simile is a comparison using *like* or *as*.

Read the selection. Answer the questions below.

It seems as if everyone has some chore they hate to do. Getting them to do it is *like pulling teeth*. For my sister, it's doing dishes. For my brother, it's taking out the trash. For me, it's cleaning my room.

❶ Is something being compared to something else? ◯ yes ◯ no

❷ Is the word *like* or *as* used to compare? ◯ yes ◯ no

❸ Are the words *like pulling teeth* part of a simile in this example? ◯ yes ◯ no

---

Expressions That Are Metaphors

This unit highlights idioms that are metaphors. Below are two lists of metaphors. The first, *Ten to Teach*, presents the 10 metaphors introduced and taught in this unit. The second, *More to Mention*, offers additional metaphors that you may want to mention or use to create additional activities.

Ten to Teach

1. **hit the sack**
2. **the crack of dawn**
3. **bottled up**
4. **a tongue-lashing**
5. **in the dark**

6. **buttoned his lip**
7. **hands are tied**
8. **hard to swallow**
9. **stopped cold**
10. **simmer down**

More to Mention

► tower of strength
► back out
► catch off guard

► in the same boat
► spill the beans
► lips are sealed

► teacher's pet
► bag of tricks
► two-faced

Using This Unit

Begin by reading to students the basic *Ten to Teach* metaphors. First, ask students if they have ever heard or used any of these expressions, and if so, how and where. Next, tell the students that you are going to read the expressions again, and this time they are to listen for anything they have in common. Accept all answers, and then point out that all the expressions compare one thing to another. Teach or review the definition of a *metaphor*—a direct comparison. Explain to students that a metaphor is like a simile, except that it does not use the words *like* or *as* to compare.

On the next page is a story that includes the *Ten to Teach* metaphors. Note that the story is not intended to be an example of good writing; it would not be natural to use 10 metaphors in such a short piece. The purpose of the story is simply to use all the expressions in context. The story is at approximately a 2.5 reading level. Use this information to read it aloud to students, have them read it, or both. This reproducible page includes the story and questions for students to answer related to the metaphors used.

The final five pages of the unit introduce the basic *Ten to Teach* metaphors individually, two to a page. These can be reproduced as is, or cut apart into separate cards. Note: As in the previous unit on similes, in this unit students are asked questions that lead them to decide if a phrase in a selection is used as a metaphor or not.

Optional: Use one of the ideas or activities in the introductory section of this book as an extension or follow-up to the unit.

Expressions That Are Metaphors *(cont.)*

Name _____ Date _____

Below is a story containing 13 metaphors. Can you tell what they mean?

Last night I decided to read before I **hit the sack**. I must have fallen asleep in the middle of the mystery. So, I continued the story in my dream....

It was the darkest part of the night—the time just before **the crack of dawn**. They were behind a bush and looking right at the rickety old house. Was it really haunted? Des wanted to know for sure. Carlos was scared. So far he had kept his fears **bottled up**, but now he began to shiver and stammer. Des turned to Carlos and gave him **a tongue-lashing**. **"Simmer down**, kid. They might hear us!"

Carlos was **in the dark** about who or what "they" might be. He was pretty sure, though, that he didn't want them to hear him, so he **buttoned his lip**.

"This is it," said Des, who was a **tower of strength**. "It's too late to **back out** now. Our **hands are tied**. The only thing to do now is sneak in and **catch them off guard**."

Carlos found the words **hard to swallow**, but when Des began to creep toward the house, he followed. Just as they approached the house, something **stopped them cold**. But what?

Just then my alarm went off.   Maybe I'll finish the story in my dream tonight.

Read or listen to the story again. Then answer these questions about the metaphors. To help you find them, the metaphors are in **dark print** in the text.

1. Circle the metaphor you could use in place of *stopped them cold*.
   a. made them freeze in their tracks
   b. turned them to ice
   c. gave them cold feet

2. What in the story was *hard to swallow*? _____

3. What in the story was *bottled up*? _____

4. Rewrite each of these statements so that it contains a metaphor:

I went to bed. _____

He stopped talking. _____

We can't do anything. _____

Name _____ Date _____

Metaphor ▶ hit the sack

Meaning ▶ go to bed

How It Is Used ▶ Up until the second day of our cruise, the water was calm. But once the storm hit, it really rocked the boat all night. There was nothing to do but **hit the sack**. The next morning, many passengers complained that they were seasick.

Recognizing Metaphors ▶ Remember: A metaphor is a direct comparison (without the words *like* or *as*).

Read the selection. Answer the questions below.

More than anything, Kenny wanted a set of drums for Christmas. When he saw a large sack under the tree, his hopes went up that he had gotten his wish. While his parents weren't looking, he gently *hit the sack* with his foot. His eyes lit up as he felt the bed of the bass drum.

❶ Is something being compared to something else? ○ yes ○ no

❷ Is the word *like* or *as* used to compare? ○ yes ○ no

❸ Are the words *hit the sack* part of a metaphor in this example? ○ yes ○ no

---

Metaphor ▶ the crack of dawn

Meaning ▶ sunrise

How It Is Used ▶ Luke and his grandfather went fishing on the Sandy River at **the crack of dawn**. Soon after sunrise, Luke hooked a huge trout and his grandfather helped him reel it in. "What a catch!" his grandfather exclaimed.

Recognizing Metaphors ▶ Remember: A metaphor is a direct comparison (without the words *like* or *as*).

Read the selection. Answer the questions below.

It was the *crack of dawn* when Dylan looked out the window and saw his neighbor's dog digging up the tulip bulbs his mother had just planted.

❶ Is something being compared to something else? ○ yes ○ no

❷ Is the word *like* or *as* used to compare? ○ yes ○ no

❸ Are the words *crack of dawn* part of a metaphor in this example? ○ yes ○ no

---

Name _____ Date _____

Metaphor ▶ **bottled up**

Meaning ▶ **keep contained; keep feelings to oneself**

How It Is Used ▶ The soccer referee held up a yellow card. This was a signal to warn Nick about his unsportsmanlike behavior. Nick decided to keep his feelings **bottled up** and stayed focused on following the rules so he could stay in the game.

Recognizing Metaphors ▶ Remember: A metaphor is a direct comparison (without the words *like* or *as*).

Read the selection. Answer the questions below.

Mike and his dad were talking about sports. Mike said that he had always wanted to learn to surf. "I don't want you to take up surfing until you're older," his dad said. "It is just too dangerous." Mike *bottled up* his disappointment because he knew his dad was right.

❶ Is something being compared to something else? ◯ yes ◯ no

❷ Is the word *like* or *as* used to compare? ◯ yes ◯ no

❸ Are the words *bottled up* part of a metaphor in this example? ◯ yes ◯ no

---

Metaphor ▶ **a tongue-lashing**

Meaning ▶ **scold; to correct someone harshly**

How It Is Used ▶ When Mrs. Jackson saw Emily's cell phone bill, she got mad. She thought about giving her daughter **a tongue-lashing**, but she decided that wouldn't help. Instead, she decided to make Emily use her own money to help pay the bill.

Recognizing Metaphors ▶ Remember: A metaphor is a direct comparison (without the words *like* or *as*).

Read the selection. Answer the questions below.

Andrew knew that he had disobeyed his dad and deserved to be scolded. So he took his dad's *tongue-lashing* without talking back. Andrew hoped that he wouldn't be grounded as well.

❶ Is something being compared to something else? ◯ yes ◯ no

❷ Is the word *like* or *as* used to compare? ◯ yes ◯ no

❸ Are the words *tongue-lashing* part of a metaphor in this example? ◯ yes ◯ no

---

Name _____ Date _____

Metaphor ▶ **in the dark**

Meaning ▶ **without knowing or understanding; lacking information**

How It Is Used ▶ When Dawn came into the den, her mom and dad were looking at a map. "Come help us make our summer vacation plans," Dawn's mom said. "This is one time when you don't want to be **in the dark**."

Recognizing Metaphors ▶ Remember: A metaphor is a direct comparison (without the words *like* or *as*).

Read the selection. Answer the questions below.

Bailey dreads being alone *in the dark*. So, she keeps a nightlight on in her bedroom at night to make her feel safe.

❶ Is something being compared to something else? ○ yes ○ no

❷ Is the word *like* or *as* used to compare? ○ yes ○ no

❸ Are the words *in the dark* part of a metaphor in this example? ○ yes ○ no

---

Metaphor ▶ **button one's lip**

Meaning ▶ **stop talking; be silent or quiet**

How It Is Used ▶ Brett and Conner were blowing up balloons for Alex's surprise birthday party. When Alex walked in, Brett whispered to Conner. "**Button your lip**," he said. "We don't want Alex to suspect that we are giving her a surprise party."

Recognizing Metaphors ▶ Remember: A metaphor is a direct comparison (without the words *like* or *as*).

Read the selection. Answer the questions below.

I was about to march in my first parade. My new band uniform was bright red and had six shiny buttons down the front of the jacket. When I looked down and saw a missing *button, my lip* started to quiver. There was no time to fix it as it was time for the parade to begin.

❶ Is something being compared to something else? ○ yes ○ no

❷ Is the word *like* or *as* used to compare? ○ yes ○ no

❸ Are the words *button my lip* part of a metaphor in this example? ○ yes ○ no

---

Name _____ **Date** _____

Metaphor ▶ **hands are tied**

Meaning ▶ **unable to act on something; out of one's control**

How It Is Used ▶ When I heard the ice cream truck at the park, I asked my mom for money. She said her wallet was at home. "I'd like to buy you a treat, but my **hands are tied**; I have no money," my mom said. "I'll get you some ice cream later."

Recognizing Metaphors ▶ Remember: A metaphor is a direct comparison (without the words *like* or *as*).

Read the selection. Answer the questions below.

As he sat in the dentist's waiting room, Rodney was nervous. He gripped the chair so hard that it seemed like his *hands were tied to* it. "Relax," said his brother as he handed him a comic book.

❶ Is something being compared to something else? ◯ yes ◯ no

❷ Is the word *like* or *as* used to compare? ◯ yes ◯ no

❸ Are the words *hands were tied* part of a metaphor in this example? ◯ yes ◯ no

---

Metaphor ▶ **hard to swallow**

Meaning ▶ **difficult to accept or believe**

How It Is Used ▶ My sister told me that she had bought me a gift while she was on vacation, but that she lost it on the way home. I found her story **hard to swallow**, since I know my sister is always very careful with things she buys with her own money.

Recognizing Metaphors ▶ Remember: A metaphor is a direct comparison (without the words *like* or *as*).

Read the selection. Answer the questions below.

It was really *hard to swallow* the large vitamin each morning. Mom saw that I was having a hard time, so we decided to switch to a brand that was smaller and easier to take.

❶ Is something being compared to something else? ◯ yes ◯ no

❷ Is the word *like* or *as* used to compare? ◯ yes ◯ no

❸ Are the words *hard to swallow* part of a metaphor in this example? ◯ yes ◯ no

---

Expressions That Are Metaphors *(cont.)*

Name _____ Date _____

Metaphor ▶ stopped cold

Meaning ▶ stopped in an instant, as if frozen; ceased immediately

How It Is Used ▶ I opened the front door one evening and **stopped cold**. Sitting on my front porch was a large raccoon. I had never seen a raccoon up close before—and certainly didn't expect to see one on my front porch!

Recognizing Metaphors ▶ Remember: A metaphor is a direct comparison (without the words *like* or *as*).

Read the selection. Answer the questions below.

My sister and I looked both ways before we started to walk across the street. But as soon as we stepped off the curb, we *stopped cold* as a motorcycle rounded the corner and sped past us.

❶ Is something being compared to something else? ○ yes ○ no

❷ Is the word *like* or *as* used to compare? ○ yes ○ no

❸ Are the words *stopped cold* part of a metaphor in this example? ○ yes ○ no

---

Metaphor ▶ simmer down

Meaning ▶ calm down; chill out

How It Is Used ▶ Our dogs always bark and bark when someone they don't know comes to the door. We have to get them to **simmer down** before we invite our guests in.

Recognizing Metaphors ▶ Remember: A metaphor is a direct comparison (without the words *like* or *as*).

Read the selection. Answer the questions below.

My little brother always gets so excited when his birthday is coming. Even two weeks before, we have to tell him to *simmer down* and be patient to celebrate his big day.

❶ Is something being compared to something else? ○ yes ○ no

❷ Is the word *like* or *as* used to compare? ○ yes ○ no

❸ Are the words *simmer down* part of a metaphor in this example? ○ yes ○ no

Expressions That Exaggerate (Hyperbole)

This unit highlights expressions that are exaggerations (hyperbole). Below are two lists of expressions. The first, *Ten to Teach*, presents the 10 examples introduced and taught in this unit. The second, *More to Mention*, offers additional examples that you may want to mention or use to create additional activities.

Ten to Teach

1. crying one's eyes out
2. make one's head spin
3. a dime a dozen
4. worth its weight in gold
5. talking one's head off

6. run/running ragged
7. all ears
8. every trick in the book
9. in a split second
10. bursting at the seams

More to Mention

▶ go through the roof
▶ back-breaking work
▶ die of boredom
▶ all thumbs

▶ in no time
▶ die laughing
▶ up to one's neck
▶ out of this world

▶ bored stiff
▶ like nothing on earth

Using This Unit

Begin by reading to students the basic *Ten to Teach* expressions. First, ask students if they have ever heard or used any of these expressions, and if so, how and where. Next, tell the students that you are going to read the expressions again, and this time they are to listen for anything they have in common. Accept all answers, and then point out that all the expressions exaggerate, or say something that could never be true as described. If you like, tell students that this type of expression is called a *hyperbole*. Read the list once more. Ask students what part of each expression could never be true as stated.

On the next page is a story that includes the *Ten to Teach* expressions that exaggerate. Note that the story is not intended to be an example of good writing; it would not be natural to use 10 exaggerations in such a short piece. The purpose of the story is simply to use all the expressions in context. The story is at approximately a 2.9 reading level. Use this information to read it aloud to students, have them read it, or both. This reproducible page includes the story and questions for students to answer related to the expressions used.

The final five pages of the unit introduce the basic *Ten to Teach* expressions individually, two to a page. These can be reproduced as is, or cut apart into separate cards. Use these after the story to reinforce the meanings of these expressions or to test students' understanding of them. Or, use them before the story as preparation for reading or for scaffolding as needed.

Optional: Use one of the ideas or activities in the introductory section of this book as an extension or follow-up to the unit.

Name _____ Date _____

Below is a story containing 10 expressions that exaggerate. Can you tell what they mean?

> Anna spent the night **crying her eyes out**. She had heard her parents talking about moving to another state. The thought of it **made her head spin**. What would she ever do without her best friend, Emma? "Most friends are **a dime a dozen**," she thought. "But Emma is **worth her weight in gold**."
>
> The next morning, Anna was quiet at breakfast. No one noticed though, because her brother Sam was **talking his head off** as usual. Mom was **running ragged** trying to get herself and the family out the door. Anna just ate and left for school.
>
> When she got there, Emma asked what was wrong. She was **all ears** when Anna told her what she heard. Afterward, it took **every trick in the book** for the girls to get through the day.
>
> That night at dinner, Dad said he had something to tell everyone. Anna took a deep breath. "Your mom and I have some news. Grandma is getting older. We have been talking about moving up north to be closer to where she lives."
>
> Anna squeezed her eyes shut as her dad continued. "But we have decided we would rather stay put and have Grandma move in here with us."
>
> **In a split second**, Anna went from sad to happy. She wasn't moving after all! She was **bursting at the seams** to give Emma the news. They could still be best friends! Now and forever!

Read or listen to the story again. Then answer these questions about the expressions. To help you find them, the exaggerations are in **dark print** in the text.

1. The girls used *every trick in the book* to get through the day. What do you think this sentence means? _____

   _____

   _____

2. In your own words, explain what *exaggeration* means. _____

   _____

3. Anna's mood changed in a *split second*. Describe a time when your mood changed in a split second, and why. _____

   _____

   _____

Name _____ Date _____

Hyperbole ▶ **cry one's eyes out**

Meaning ▶ **crying for a long time; being very upset**

How It Is Used ▶ One day while Kelly was at school, her dog got out. She put up Lost Dog signs everywhere. Kelly **cried her eyes out**, thinking that Barkley was gone forever. Two days later, he just showed up at the door!

Recognizing Hyperbole ▶ Remember: Hyperbole is an expression that exaggerates, or describes something as greatly more or less than it really is, and could not actually be true.

Read the selection. Answer the questions below.

Mrs. Porter's brother was injured in a car accident. Although the doctor said that he would be fine after a while, she *cried her eyes out* until he started to get better.

❶ What does the phrase *cried her eyes out* here describe? ○ crying ○ eyes

❷ Is something described in a way that could not actually be true? ○ yes ○ no

❸ Does the description use hyperbole? ○ yes ○ no

Hyperbole ▶ **make one's head spin**

Meaning ▶ **to think about something that is confusing or overwhelming**

How It Is Used ▶ When Vincent first came to the United States, everything seemed so confusing. For example, the first time he bought cereal at the store, all the choices **made his head spin**.

Recognizing Hyperbole ▶ Remember: Hyperbole is an expression that exaggerates, or describes something as greatly more or less than it really is, and could not actually be true.

Read the selection. Answer the questions below.

Paul was looking at all the new toys in the toy store. He picked up a toy robot. According to the package, when you push his button, the motor *makes his head spin*!

❶ What does the phrase *makes his head spin* here describe? ○ thinking ○ spinning

❷ Is something described in a way that could not actually be true? ○ yes ○ no

❸ Does the description use hyperbole? ○ yes ○ no

Name _____ Date _____

Hyperbole ▶	**a dime a dozen**
Meaning ▶	**very cheap; inexpensive; not worth much**
How It Is Used ▶	Jonathan has a collection of figurines from popular movies. He had three of the same one, so he offered to trade Marsha for one he didn't have. But she answered, "No way. That's not a good deal. Those are a **dime a dozen**."
Recognizing Hyperbole ▶	Remember: Hyperbole is an expression that exaggerates, or describes something as greatly more or less than it really is, and could not actually be true.

Read the selection. Answer the questions below.

Danny looked at all the candy. Jelly beans were only *a dime a dozen*, so he bought a handful.

❶ What does the phrase *a dime a dozen* here describe? ◯ the cost of the candy ◯ the popularity of the candy

❷ Is something described in a way that could not actually be true? ◯ yes ◯ no

❸ Does the description use hyperbole? ◯ yes ◯ no

Hyperbole ▶	**worth its weight in gold**
Meaning ▶	**very valuable; very important or appreciated**
How It Is Used ▶	On the way home from the circus, the Feltons talked about the acts. Chris said, "I liked the juggler best." Susan said, "The elephants were my favorite." Dad said, "They were good, but the lion tamer's act was **worth its weight in gold**!"
Recognizing Hyperbole ▶	Remember: Hyperbole is an expression that exaggerates, or describes something as greatly more or less than it really is, and could not actually be true.

Read the selection. Answer the questions below.

On Father's Day, Mr. Penn opened a gift from his two children. He smiled and said, "This is a very nice tie, but the card you two made is *worth its weight in gold*."

❶ What does the phrase *worth its weight in gold* here describe?
◯ the cost of the card ◯ what the card means to Dad

❷ Is something described in a way that could not actually be true? ◯ yes ◯ no

❸ Does the description use hyperbole? ◯ yes ◯ no

Name _____ Date _____

Hyperbole ▶ **talking one's head off**

Meaning ▶ **talking for a long time or nonstop**

How It Is Used ▶ I enjoyed our field trip, but our tour guide really **talked his head off** about the museum's founder.

Recognizing Hyperbole ▶ Remember: Hyperbole is an expression that exaggerates, or describes something as greatly more or less than it really is, and could not actually be true.

Read the selection. Answer the questions below.

When Brad got home from the trip to the amusement park, he told us about his day. He liked everything, but he *talked his head off* about the Monster Coaster.

❶ What does the phrase *talked his head off* here describe? ◯ Brad's head ◯ talking

❷ Is something described in a way that could not actually be true? ◯ yes ◯ no

❸ Does the description use hyperbole? ◯ yes ◯ no

Hyperbole ▶ **run/running ragged**

Meaning ▶ **to keep someone busy to the point of being tired and worn out**

How It Is Used ▶ When my cousin was planning her wedding, she had everyone **running ragged** to get things ready.

Recognizing Hyperbole ▶ Remember: Hyperbole is an expression that exaggerates, or describes something as greatly more or less than it really is, and could not actually be true.

Read the selection. Answer the questions below.

After two years, Jason's favorite baseball shirt started to rip. Mom tried to get him to use his new baseball shirt, but he preferred to *run ragged* from base to base.

❶ What does the phrase *run ragged* here describe? ◯ a torn shirt ◯ being tired

❷ Is something described in a way that could not actually be true? ◯ yes ◯ no

❸ Does the description use hyperbole? ◯ yes ◯ no

Name _____ Date _____

Hyperbole ▶	**all ears**
Meaning ▶	**listening very closely; very interested in what is being said**
How It Is Used ▶	My little brother doesn't usually pay attention when I talk about anything. He must like my friend Christie, though, because he is **all ears** when I mention her.
Recognizing Hyperbole ▶	Remember: Hyperbole is an expression that exaggerates, or describes something as greatly more or less than it really is, and could not actually be true.

Read the selection. Answer the questions below.

Kathy and her mother were buying cat food. At the checkout, Kathy picked up a bag of strange-looking things. She asked what they were. The clerk said, "They are for dogs to chew. The big bag is pigs' feet. The one you are holding is *all ears*." Kathy made a face and put it down.

❶ What does the phrase *all ears* describe here? ◯ ears ◯ listening

❷ Is something described in a way that could not actually be true? ◯ yes ◯ no

❸ Does the description use hyperbole? ◯ yes ◯ no

Hyperbole ▶	**every trick in the book**
Meaning ▶	**every way possible one can think of to get or do something**
How It Is Used ▶	Bill wanted a new electronic game. He had just gotten a new game for his birthday, so he knew it would take **every trick in the book** to convince his parents to buy another one.
Recognizing Hyperbole ▶	Remember: Hyperbole is an expression that exaggerates, or describes something as greatly more or less than it really is, and could not actually be true.

Read the selection. Answer the questions below.

Ruth wanted to amaze her friends. She got a book of magic tricks from the library. She learned *every trick in the book*.

❶ What does the phrase *every trick in the book* here describe?
◯ tricks in a book   ◯ figuring out something

❷ Is something described in a way that could not actually be true? ◯ yes ◯ no

❸ Does the description use hyperbole? ◯ yes ◯ no

 #50158—*Idioms and Other English Expressions*

Name _____ Date _____

Hyperbole ▶ in a split second

Meaning ▶ very, very quickly

How It Is Used ▶ Ron was great at math. He learned all the basic addition facts and subtraction facts in just a couple of days. Ask Ron any basic fact and he can answer correctly **in a split second**.

Recognizing Hyperbole ▶ Remember: Hyperbole is an expression that exaggerates, or describes something as greatly more or less than it really is, and could not actually be true.

Read the selection. Answer the questions below.

The race cars sat at the start line. When the flag dropped, they all took off in a blur. They went so fast that the race was over *in a split second*.

❶ What does the phrase *in a split second* here describe? ◯ speed ◯ part of a second

❷ Is something described in a way that could not actually be true? ◯ yes ◯ no

❸ Does the description use hyperbole? ◯ yes ◯ no

Hyperbole ▶ bursting at the seams

Meaning ▶ very excited or proud; anxious to say or do something

How It Is Used ▶ Last year at the fair, Rita was not tall enough for some rides. This year, she was **bursting at the seams** as she stood next to the height sign at the fair and saw that she measured up.

Recognizing Hyperbole ▶ Remember: Hyperbole is an expression that exaggerates, or describes something as greatly more or less than it really is, and could not actually be true.

Read the selection. Answer the questions below.

Phil was *bursting at the seams* to tell his mom and dad he had won the spelling competition.

❶ What does the phrase *bursting at the seams* here describe?

◯ clothes coming apart   ◯ anxious to do something

❷ Is something described in a way that could not actually be true? ◯ yes ◯ no

❸ Does the description use hyperbole? ◯ yes ◯ no

Just Common Sayings (Proverbs)

This unit highlights expressions that are proverbs. Proverbs are common sayings that apply to a variety of situations. Below are two lists of proverbs. The first, *Ten to Teach*, presents the 10 proverbs introduced and taught in this unit. The second, *More to Mention*, offers additional proverbs that you may want to mention or use to create additional activities.

Ten to Teach

1. **Two heads are better than one.**
2. **Out of sight, out of mind.**
3. **Actions speak louder than words.**
4. **Don't judge a book by its cover.**
5. **Look before you leap.**
6. **Put your best foot forward.**
7. **Don't cry over spilled milk.**
8. **Don't put the cart before the horse.**
9. **Don't count your chickens before they hatch.**
10. **The early bird catches the worm.**

More to Mention

- Cat got your tongue?
- Variety is the spice of life.
- Finders keepers, losers weepers.
- A stitch in time saves nine.
- Better late than never
- Caught between a rock and a hard place
- Where there's a will, there's a way.
- Time flies when you are having fun.

Using This Unit

Begin by reading to students the proverbs from the *Ten to Teach* list. As you read, ask students if they have ever heard or used any of these proverbs, and if so, how and where. Next, explain to students that proverbs are common sayings. Like idioms, the words do not mean what they actually say, but express truth, advice, or wisdom about a variety of situations.

On the next two pages is a list of possible meanings for the *Ten to Teach* proverbs. Note that the meanings given are not intended to be precise definitions. You will want to have students offer their own interpretations of the proverbs. You can use this page for your own reference to discuss the proverbs, or it can be reproduced for students. If used as student pages, there is a place for them to mark which proverbs they have heard or used themselves.

The final four pages of this special unit offer a series of stories, each of which could end with a proverb. On each reproducible page, three of the *Ten to Teach* proverbs and two situational stories are given. Students read or listen to each situation and then choose the appropriate proverb to add to the end of story. By completing all four pages, students will have analyzed the *Ten to Teach* proverbs and used context to apply the correct one.

Optional: Use one of the ideas or activities in the introductory section of this book as an extension or follow-up to the unit.

Name _____ **Date** _____

Below are some expressions called proverbs. Proverbs are common sayings. Like idioms, the words do not actually mean what they say, but they express truth, advice, or wisdom about a variety of situations. Read each of the 10 proverbs and their meanings. Put a ✔ by any that you have heard or used yourself. Be ready to describe a situation in which you heard or used it.

Proverb ▶ _____ **Two heads are better than one.**

Meaning ▶ Two people thinking or working together can often accomplish more than one person alone.

Proverb ▶ _____ **Out of sight, out of mind.**

Meaning ▶ It's easy to forget about something when it is not right in front of you.

Proverb ▶ _____ **Actions speak louder than words.**

Meaning ▶ What a person does means more than what he or she says.

Proverb ▶ _____ **Don't judge a book by its cover.**

Meaning ▶ The outside of something or someone doesn't show what's on the inside.

Proverb ▶ _____ **Look before you leap.**

Meaning ▶ Don't do something without knowing what you are getting into and thinking about it first.

Name _____ Date _____

Proverb ▶ _____ **Put your best foot forward.**

Meaning ▶ Show others the best you can be or do.

Proverb ▶ _____ **Don't cry over spilled milk.**

Meaning ▶ Don't worry or be upset over something that is already done.

Proverb ▶ _____ **Don't put the cart before the horse.**

Meaning ▶ Don't do things in the wrong order.

Proverb ▶ _____ **Don't count your chickens before they hatch.**

Meaning ▶ Don't count on having something before you actually get it.

Proverb ▶ _____ **The early bird catches the worm.**

Meaning ▶ The person who does things as soon as possible usually benefits.

#50158—Idioms and Other English Expressions

Name _____ Date _____

Pick the Proverbs Part 1

Proverbs, like idioms, do not actually mean what they say. They are meant to express truth, advice, or wisdom. Read each story. Choose the proverb that best fits at the end. Write it on the line.

Out of sight, out of mind.

Don't cry over spilled milk.

Two heads are better than one.

Story 1

I heard Dad talking to himself in the kitchen. He always grumbles out loud when he loses something.

"What are you looking for?" I said cheerfully.

"Oh, the garage key...again!" he answered. "I saw it here just a little while ago. Now it is gone and I have been looking all over for it."

"Why don't I help you find it?" I volunteered. "After all, _____

_____

Story 2

Kevin had homework to do. "I'll finish after soccer practice," he thought to himself. "There will be plenty of time left."

The team had a good practice. The coach said they could stay and have pizza if they wanted to. Everybody stayed. After they ate, they talked and kicked the ball around some more. Before they knew it, it was 8 o'clock.

When Kevin got home, he saw his forgotten homework right where he left it.

"Uh-oh," he said. "I guess it was a case of _____

_____

Name _____ Date _____

Pick the Proverbs Part 2

Proverbs, like idioms, do not actually mean what they say. They are meant to express truth, advice, or wisdom. Read each story. Choose the proverb that best fits at the end. Write it on the line.

Don't judge a book by its cover.

Don't put the cart before the horse.

Actions speak louder than words.

Story 3

Carrie wanted to be the best at something. She tried learning to play the piano, but gave up after just a few weeks. She signed up for swimming lessons, but quit because the water was cold.

One day she was baking cookies with her grandmother. "I want to be the best baker in the world!" she declared.

Grandma smiled. "Carrie, you have said that you wanted to be the best piano player, the best swimmer, and the best baker. But these things take time and you don't stick to it. If you really want to be the best at something, you need to be patient and work hard. _____

_____

Story 4

Ray was in the library looking for a book. Suddenly, an older boy came down the same aisle that Ray was in. The boy was wearing the same T-shirt as one of the boys who had bullied Ray on the bus. The older boy came toward Ray. "Back off!" Ray said as tough as he could.

"Whoa, kid," said the older boy. "I am just looking for a book!"

"Oh, sorry," said Ray. He felt silly. Then he thought to himself, " _____

_____

Name _____ Date _____

Pick the Proverbs Part 3

Proverbs, like idioms, do not actually mean what they say. They are meant to express truth, advice, or wisdom. Read each story. Choose the proverb that best fits at the end. Write it on the line.

Look before you leap.

Don't count your chickens before they hatch.

The early bird caches the worm.

Story 5

Laura liked to design things on the computer with clip art and special type. She made a card for her mother. Her mother said it was beautiful and that it was as pretty as a card bought from a store.

Laura replied with excitement, "Maybe I could earn some extra money selling cards! I'll charge a dollar a card. Everyone will buy them. In no time, I'll have lots of money!"

Her mother said, "Yes, you may be able to make a few sales, but _____

_____

Story 6

Ira's dad told Ira that he could get a kitten. On Friday the pet store had pet adoptions. They went and looked at the kittens. They were all so cute that Ira couldn't decide which one to take. He asked his dad if they could go get some ice cream while he thought about it.

Dad agreed and they left. While Ira ate his ice cream, he decided on the black and white one with the spot on his nose. But when they returned to the pet store, Ira couldn't find the one he wanted. He was told that someone adopted him while they were gone. Dad put his arm around Ira. "Sorry, son, but _____

_____

Name _____ Date _____

Pick the Proverbs Part 4

Proverbs, like idioms, do not actually mean what they say. They are meant to epress truth, advice, or wisdom. Read each story. Choose the proverb that best fits at the end. Write it on the line.

Don't cry over spilled milk.

Look before you leap.

Put your best foot forward.

Story 7

Rosie's family always recycles. When the school asked for volunteers to go around the neighborhood to tell people about recycling and collecting cans, newspapers, and bottles, Rosie raised her hand. On Saturday she happily started going from house to house. At about the third stop, she already had way more than she could carry in the bag she brought. At the fourth house, the man had a stack of newspapers. He saw her problem and offered to lend her his son's wagon. "Rosie, next time you start something, you will want to plan ahead. It's good to _____

_____

Story 8

Uncle Dean was coming for dinner. The last time Shane saw his Uncle Dean, he admired his baseball cap with the fancy team logo. He talked about it so much that Uncle Dean gave it to him. Then, a couple of weeks later, Shane lost it. He felt terrible.

When Uncle Dean arrived, Shane knew he would ask about the cap. So, before he asked, Shane told Uncle Dean what happened.

"It's OK, Shane," he said. "I know you feel bad about it, but _____

_____

Many of the answers will show an example of how the students might respond. For many of the questions there may be more than one correct answer.

Page 8
Answers will vary.

Page 11
Answers will vary.

Page 13
Answers will vary.

Page 19
1. blue
2. a long time
3. embarrassed
4. probably yes; reasons will vary
5. not expecting it

Page 20
once in a blue moon: 2
out of the blue: 1

Page 21
caught red-handed: 2
red-faced: 1

Page 22
green with envy: 1
green-eyed monster: 1

Page 23
tickled pink: 2
red-carpet treatment: 1

Page 24
looking/feeling blue: 1
silver lining: 2

Page 26
1. squirrel
2. eager/alert, lively
3. told the secret
4. Answers will vary.
5. snake in the grass
6. Answers will vary.

Page 27
let the cat out of the bag: 2
clam up: 2

Page 28
bright-eyed and bushy-tailed: 2
bugged/bug off: 1

Page 29
butterflies in one's stomach: 2
snake in the grass: 1

Page 30
in the doghouse: 1
hold your horses: 2

Page 31
monkey business: 2
hear a peep: 1

Page 33
1. Yes. He thought it would be a piece of cake.
2. A person with a sweet tooth likes sugary foods.
3. No, Dad does not take Mom's temper very seriously.
4. It's bad to be chewed out.
5. Answers will vary, but may include that Mom wished that she could take back what she said.

Page 34
piece of cake: 2
chew out/get chewed out: 1

Page 35
a sweet tooth: 2
doesn't grow on trees: 2

Page 36
going bananas: 1
take with a grain of salt: 2

Page 37
butter someone up: 1
in a nutshell: 1

Page 38
food for thought: 1
eat one's words: 2

Page 40
1. They see very well. Answers may vary, but this is the best response.
2. They disagree.
3. He probably felt disappointed; answers will vary.
4. Plain as the nose on your face means in plain sight.
5. Answers will vary, although no is the likely response.

Page 41
eagle-eyed: 1
keep one's eyes peeled: 1

Page 42
see eye to eye: 2
fall upon deaf ears: 1

Page 43
didn't bat an eyelash: 2
eyes in the back of one's head: 2

Page 44
put one's nose to the grindstone: 2
nose around: 2

Page 45
plain as the nose on one's face: 1
pull the wool over one's eyes: 1

Page 47
1. nervous, scared, troubled, excited, anxious, worried
2. Answers will vary, but will involve reporting someone cheating.
3. Answers will vary.
4. Answers will vary.

Page 48
blow the whistle: 2
rock the boat: 2

Page 49
bite one's tongue: 1
get off the hook: 2

Page 50
draw the line: 2
hit the nail on the head: 2

Page 51
carry the ball: 1
get to the bottom of: 2

Page 52
chill out: 2
catch you later: 1

Page 54
1. keep it a secret
2. Answers will vary.
3. a. continue; b. enjoy; c. annoys; d. wish

Page 55
get a kick out of: 2
get under one's skin: 2

Page 56
get the runaround: 2
get over it: 2

Page 57
get cold feet: 1
keep it under wraps: 2

Page 58

keep one's cool: 2

keep one's fingers crossed: 1

Page 59

keep the ball rolling: 2

keep a straight face: 2

Page 61

1. You are saying something bad or disrespectful.

2. kidding

3. sure

4. getting a favor

5. know what it is

6. -ing

Page 62

pull a stunt: 2

put one's foot in one's mouth: 2

Page 63

pull one's leg: 1

put someone down: 2

Page 64

put in a good word: 1

pull some strings: 1

Page 65

put one's money where one's mouth is: 1

put one's finger on it: 1

Page 66

pull one in: 1

put it/one to the test: 1

Page 68

1. yes; Answers will vary.

2. like

3. a. getting Paul to play;
   b. how Paul walked;
   c. kicking

4. a. Answers will vary.

Page 69

like two peas in a pod: no, no, no; as different as night and day: yes, yes, yes

Page 70

like a bump on a log: yes, yes, yes

as quiet as a mouse: no, no, no

Page 71

like a fish out of water: yes, yes, yes

as easy as pie: no, no, no

Page 72

as stiff as a board: yes, yes, yes

feel like two cents: yes, yes, yes

Page 73

fit like a glove: no, no, no

like pulling teeth: yes, yes, yes

Page 75

1. a. made them freeze in their tracks

2. words or fears

3. fears

4. I hit the sack. He buttoned his lip. Our hands are tied.

Page 76

hit the sack: no, no, no

crack of dawn: yes, no, yes

Page 77

bottled up: yes, no, yes

a tongue-lashing: yes, no, yes

Page 78

in the dark: no, no, no

button one's lip: no, no, no

Page 79

hands are tied: no, no, no

hard to swallow: no, no, no

Page 80

stopped cold: yes, no, yes

simmer down: yes, no, yes

Page 82

1. Answers will vary.

2. Answers will vary, but should include the idea of stretching the truth.

3. Answers will vary.

Page 83

cry one's eyes out: crying, yes, yes

make one's head spin: spinning, no, no

Page 84

a dime a dozen: the cost of the candy, no, no

worth its weight in gold: what the card means to Dad, yes, yes

Page 85

talking one's head off: talking, yes, yes

run/running ragged: a torn shirt, no, no

Page 86

all ears: ears, no, no

every trick in the book: tricks in a book, no, no

Page 87

in a split second: speed, yes, yes

bursting at the seams: anxious to do something, yes, yes

Pages 89 and 90

Answers will vary.

Page 91

Story 1: Two heads are better than one.

Story 2: Out of sight, out of mind.

Page 92

Story 3: Actions speak louder than words.

Story 4: Don't judge a book by its cover.

Page 93

Story 5: Don't count your chickens before they hatch.

Story 6: The early bird catches the worm.

Page 94

Story 7: Look before you leap.

Story 8: Don't cry over spilled milk.